"One mark of C. S. Lewis's achievement is the number of insightful books inspired by him that keep appearing. *Removing the Dragon Skin* records his transformative impact on the author's life and thought, especially with respect to the problem of low spiritual self-esteem. He explores both the causes of, and remedies for, this common disabling condition, and shows how overcoming it can lead to a more profound love for God. The highest praise I can give this book is that it is one, I think, Lewis himself would have enjoyed reading!"

—Robert Banks, Fuller Theological Seminary

"In *Removing the Dragon Skin*, Braudrick courageously shares the difficulties of his life, intertwining it with his astounding knowledge of the works of Lewis. He unveils not only Lewis's mind, but also his heart, transforming long-held religious strongholds into freedom to enjoy the Savior Lewis knew so well. If a person is fortunate, they get to have a few soul-enlightening moments in life. This was one of them for me. I'm deeply grateful for it."

—Rene Gutteridge, novelist and screenwriter

"Mingled with the brilliance of C. S. Lewis, you will read Jeremiah's journey to renewed 'spiritual' self-esteem and a clearer picture of God's love. You will find it hard to put this book down!"

—Marty Grubbs, Pastor, Crossings Community Church

"Jeremiah articulates his journey through shame and into the knowing place of God's longing to be in relationship with him. One of love and friendship. And Jeremiah uses the gifted writing of one of the all-time best writers we've ever had the privilege of reading—C. S. Lewis."

—Sandi Patty Peslis, Christian artist and C. S. Lewis fan

Removing the Dragon Skin

Removing the Dragon Skin

How C. S. Lewis Helped Me Get Over My Low
Spiritual Self-Esteem and Fall Back in Love with God

JEREMIAH C. BRAUDRICK

WIPF & STOCK · Eugene, Oregon

REMOVING THE DRAGON SKIN
How C. S. Lewis Helped Me Get Over My Low Spiritual Self-Esteem and Fall Back
in Love with God

Wipf & Stock
An Imprint of Wipf and Stock Publishers
199 W. 8th Ave., Suite 3
Eugene, OR 97401

www.wipfandstock.com

PAPERBACK ISBN: 978-1-5326-7169-2
HARDCOVER ISBN: 978-1-5326-7170-8
EBOOK ISBN: 978-1-5326-7171-5

Manufactured in the U.S.A.   DECEMBER 5, 2019

To David Young

"Well, exactly the same thing happened again. And I thought to myself, oh dear, however many skins have I got to take off? . . . So I scratched away for the third time and got off a third skin, just like the two others, and stepped out of it. But as soon as I looked at myself in the water I knew it had been no good."

—EUSTACE IN *THE VOYAGE OF THE DAWN TREADER* BY C. S. LEWIS

Contents

Introduction

S OME people read C. S. Lewis today because they grew up treasuring his famous children's books, *The Chronicles of Narnia.* Perhaps they have nostalgic feelings of falling asleep to their mom's or dad's soothing voice painting beautiful pictures of a majestic lion, magical fauns, and an evil witch. They love his imagination and imagery and probably would even enjoy his science fiction novels if they came across them. Some people read Lewis because of his convincing apologetic arguments that give solidity to what they already believe or are on the verge of believing about God and the Christian experience. Others read Lewis because he's an authority on sixteenth-century English literature. Some, his poetry. Some, his allegories. Others, his skillfully crafted personal letters that he wrote to friends, family, and fans throughout his life.

For me, I found in Lewis a distant mentor. I found an unexpected cheerleader who, despite what I thought about myself, was able to convince me of what God thought about me, and how *that* is the only truth that really matters. I read Lewis because the more I do, the more I find medication for a soul who often feels beat up, often feels like a failure, often feels outside the mainstream of our Christian culture, and often feels unworthy of the grace and mercy of a loving God. For most of my life I have assumed that I was a spiritual failure. I was convinced that I was letting God down at every turn. Lewis, who is famous for his abilities to change people's minds, convinced me otherwise, even when I wasn't looking to have my low views of myself challenged.

I know I am not the only one who has suffered with some serious spiritual self-worth issues. I know there are plenty of others out there who need to be led out of a lowly spiritual condition that has been brought on by their own repeated failures, fundamentalism, addiction, self-loathing, graceless churches, or inability to follow all the current rules of our Christian culture. I know there are plenty of people like me who could use a good dose of healing and who could be reminded just how much God loves them, is proud of them, and actually likes them. If these people are anything like me and have this perpetual nagging feeling of being a "less than" Christian, then maybe Clive Staples "Jack" Lewis has something to offer them too. That's why I wrote and compiled these essays.

For brevity's sake I'll skip over any detailed biography of C. S. Lewis's life. Any Lewis fan reading this is most likely familiar with his personal life and the incredible backstory behind most of his writings, lectures, and his conversion. As for any new, would-be Lewis fans, I challenge you to pick up any number of great Lewis biographies, written by those who are far more qualified to tell his story than I. For the purposes of this book I'll simply choose to focus on some of Lewis's writings, letters, and lectures that have had a particular impact on my spiritual well-being and that have helped me find a path of healing. I'll also take readers on a journey to modern-day Oxford and Cambridge, where one can encounter Lewis's memory if one knows where to look. I do all this in hopes that someone reading this may be able to relate to my journey . . . and hopefully find some healing too. I love introducing people to C. S. Lewis who may not know much about his works beyond *The Chronicles of Narnia*. I attempt to name most of the sources I use in hopes that you will take time to explore those titles as well. At any given time, you have my complete support to put down this book and pick up one of his.

As I write this, I run a nonprofit organization that helps supply inmates with everyday essentials such as hygiene products, stamps, shoes, etc. I am also blessed to lead my church's ever-increasing prison initiatives. Because of this, a substantial number of the relationships I have in my life are people in prison and people who have been released from prison. I originally started compiling this collection of essays and Lewis-themed memoires to print out and distribute to hundreds of them. I have found that many prisoners struggle with what I will describe in this book as "low spiritual self-esteem." They often feel like a Christian, but they feel like a less-than Christian. They may know that God loves them, but sometimes they sure don't feel like it. This collection was originally intended for them—a population that I am always very anxious to introduce to Mr. C. S. Lewis. Yet after passing it around a bit, I was encouraged by some people whose academic opinions I respect to seek publishing in hopes that it may also be beneficial to a larger audience who may also struggle with spiritual self-worth. I think the fact that I was writing to an inmate population shines through from time to time, but I hope the everyday reader in the free world will also find some healing by it.

In Lewis' spiritual autobiography, *Surprised by Joy*, he suggests to the reader, who he admits may not be interested in the story of his early life, that they might be surprised they'll find some spiritual commonality with Lewis and think "What! Have you felt that too? I always thought I was the only one."[1] The same goes here. I know you probably don't know me and, because of that, really don't care about my own personal experiences . . . and that's OK. However, if you have ever felt like a third-string Christian, someone unable to perform alongside the first-stringers who seem to have got this whole Christianity thing down, then my hope is that you can relate to some of my thoughts and the way I've been able to process both Scripture and the works of C. S. Lewis. If you've experienced any sort of pain or rejection, whether it was real or something you unconsciously concocted yourself, either from strict Christian fundamentalism or just your own standards you failed to keep, or if you've ever felt like you were on the outside of those who seem to be able to please God the most, then perhaps my journey towards healing and restoration could be of benefit to you.

The reason that I chose to write in memoire and essay form, and not simply write a commentary that goes alongside Lewis's works and what you, the reader, should do in response, is because I've always lived with a "far-be-it-from-me to tell others what to do" mindset. I'm trying to figure this all out myself. So the idea of writing "Scripture says A and Lewis says B, hence you need to do C" just doesn't fit with my personality. I am much more comfortable simply presenting the evidence and letting the jury make their own conclusion.

We all have our own personal relationship with God. We're all addicts at various levels of sobriety. I wouldn't dare be so bold as to claim that I know what God wants you to do. Lewis says only "one soul in the whole of creation do you know,"[2] and that's the soul I decided to write about. It may be a flawed one. But it's who I currently am. So I decided to just tell you about my own experiences, my interpretations, some lessons I learned along the way, and some changes I have made because of my time studying C. S. Lewis . . . and if it helps someone out as a result, fantastic!

The healing that I recorded was not necessarily as clean and organized as this book lays it out, although I tried to capture it the best I could. There were several steps forward followed by several steps back. Like any real person with any real-world issues, I am a three-dimensional character. There is often more to a situation than either right or wrong. There is often more behind, "I tried 1, then 2, and the results led me to 3." We are all so much more complicated than that. Our journeys are so much messier than many step-by-step self-help books would have us believe. And that's OK. The

1. Lewis, *Surprised by Joy*, XI
2. Lewis, *Mere Christianity*, 217.

messy stories are often the best. God loves us, even in our filth. After all, he chose not to stay absent from that filth. Indeed, he removed himself from heaven and jumped square into the middle of that filth with us.

My hope is that you very much enjoy this collection of essays and memoires and find them somewhat relatable. My hope is also that you may smile a time or two. My prayer, though, is that by the end of this book I am forgotten, C. S. Lewis's works are celebrated and made relevant in your life, your battered soul finds some healing, and God gets all the glory.

PART 1

Essays on the Condition

1

Why C. S. Lewis

I have found (to my regret) that the degrees of shame and disgust which I actually feel at my own sins do not at all correspond to what my reason tells me about their comparative gravity . . . Our emotional reactions to our own behavior are of limited ethical significance.

—C. S. LEWIS, *LETTERS TO MALCOLM: CHIEFLY ON PRAYER*[1]

CHRIST says to love your enemies . . . that can be a hard command to follow when your greatest enemy has always been yourself. I generally have had no problem loving, forgiving, and praying for the vast majority of any would-be enemies: my neighbor who reported me to the HOA because I parked a boat in the street, the guy who stole my wallet and emptied my grocery account, the boss who let me go, the people that I just generally don't see eye to eye with or who rub me the wrong way. Forgiving others has always just come somewhat easy. People like me, who have struggled with self-worth issues, typically have little problem forgiving others. A low view of oneself often breeds low expectations of others . . . so, the most despised and deplorable out of all my enemies? The one person that I've had trouble even looking at during different stages of my life? The one person that I've had the highest of expectations of, yet who routinely finds ways to disappoint me? That's the man I have always struggled forgiving. That's the man that I have always had trouble giving a break and allowing grace amidst his failures. That's the man that

---

1. Lewis, *Letters to Malcom*, 99.

learning to love has always proved most difficult. The person I am talking about is, of course, myself. When one struggles to like themselves more than anyone else in this world, the commandment to love your enemies is indeed one of the hardest commands to follow. Yet the command still stands. Christ isn't specific about which enemy to love, which enemy to pray for, or which enemy to forgive. Enemies, any and all, include the man in the mirror too. I had to learn to love and forgive my enemies. I had to learn to love and forgive myself.

C. S. Lewis helped me get there. He taught me not only to love and forgive myself the way God would have me love and forgive anyone, but he taught me how to heal from this self-loathing condition, and in short, he helped me to get over myself all together. It's not about me. When one ultimately learns to accept how much God actually does love and value them, despite the flawed person living deep inside, it becomes easier to accept oneself. When we do not love and value ourselves, we are in essence disagreeing with the Creator that does. Many people spend their whole lives in this battle. Sometimes it takes the right person to come along and help them lay down their sword.

C. S. Lewis's close friend and personal secretary, Walter Hooper, says of Lewis after his death, "He was the most thoroughly converted man I have ever met."[2] Lewis is more convinced of his standing with God than anyone I have ever had the pleasure of studying. His beliefs, his actions, and his words follow where his logic led, and while he spends much of his life as an atheist, his logic eventually leads him out of it. He becomes convinced both that God is real and that he is good.

It is not emotionalism or excitement that leads Lewis to a belief in theism (although I am convinced God does accept emotional conversions towards him indeed). No, it is reason. In fact, Lewis is not emotional about it at all, let alone even excited about it. When the time comes for Lewis to surrender his life to God, he describes himself as the most reluctant and degenerate convert in all of England, a man turning towards a God that he desperately does not want to meet. He equates it to a mouse desperately not wanting to meet the cat. Yet he has to. He has to follow the reason where it leads, despite his disapproval of its eventual destination. Reluctantly, following that very reason, and the philosophical and historical evidence, Lewis kneels in his room at Magdalene College in Oxford one night, and as recorded in his spiritual autobiography *Surprised By Joy*, finally admits that God is God.[3] Only briefly, after losing his beloved wife Joy Davidman, does

2. Downing, *Most Reluctant Convert*, 160.

3. Lewis, *Surprised by Joy*, 228–29.

Lewis ever toy with the notion that God is not good,[4] a notion that he reasons himself out of and that I explore later in this book. Other than that one episode of doubt, Lewis is convinced that, not only is God good, but God loves him and accepts his flawed soul, shortcomings and all. God becomes the answer to all of this philosopher's questions. He is the answer above all other answers . . . at his face all other questions die away.[5]

This is a status and a spiritual self-confidence that I admire and have always deeply longed for. I greatly appreciate anyone who unashamedly owns their past mistakes and humanity because of the power of the cross, and who is able to boldly, without question, live in God's forgiveness, acceptance, and unconditional love. Yet unlike pre-converted Lewis, however, my biggest conflict with God has never been over his existence. I have always just kind of assumed that God was there (growing up in the buckle of the Bible Belt, I'm not sure I had a choice). Most likely stemming from my experience growing up around a fundamentalist culture and fundamentalist churches and beliefs, mixed with an occasional bout of depression, my biggest battle concerning God has always been a struggle to believe that he truly does love me, accept me, and forgive me. My biggest struggle with God has always been, not only to believe that the cross of Christ is sufficient to cover all of my mistakes, but to find freedom in that and enjoy my walk with him despite the inevitable hiccups along the way.

I've always been a thinker. Every personality test I have ever taken has told me such. I have always been a structured thinker who follows the numbers and data where they lead before I allow my heart and my emotions to follow. This has been very beneficial to me in many ways, but a handicap to me in others. The biggest way this has handicapped me has been when it comes to my walk with God. Because I am a person who makes decisions based on raw data and not emotion, I naturally assume that others do too . . . even God.

In some ways, theologically and philosophically, the redeeming power of the cross does make practical sense. I've even written several seminary papers on it: why Christ was the spotless lamb slain for our transgressions, how he fulfills the Torah, etc. But the raw data compiled by all of the mistakes in my life, the shortcomings, and the unmentionables just did not compute to someone that God could love—let alone even tolerate.

4. Lewis, *Grief Observed*, 7.
5. Lewis, *Till We Have*, 308.

Growing up I was always told that God loved me, but I also wanted him to be proud of me . . . to enjoy me . . . to like me . . . to want me in his company. I wanted to be the kind of guy that God wanted to be around and not someone who he was forced to accept because I twisted his arm by saying some magic words. Indeed, the idea of God liking me and being proud of who I was, despite the dirt in my life, just never took hold in my soul.

I am a pretty flawed individual, as the reader will no doubt understand by the time this book is finished. There have been some bumps along the way in my story. I'm an imperfect parent who has been divorced, fired, prideful, selfish, addicted, materialistic, and oh so much more. For the longest time, data has not been great. My conclusions about the spiritual state of the man in the mirror was not positive in the least. So naturally, as a thinker, I needed another, much greater, thinker to lead me out of the mental gymnastics that kept me from enjoying what Christ died to give me. I needed some help with some serious mental gymnastics. I fell in love with C. S. Lewis instantly because of this.

I've long been familiar with Lewis and had even read a Narnia book or two growing up, but it was stumbling across the quote at the beginning of this chapter from *Letters to Malcolm: Chiefly on Prayer* (a book published posthumously) in the more recent years of my life that spurred a new and profound appreciation for Lewis. Here I was introduced to a man of great intellect and deep emotional strength, but like me he seemingly placed a great deal of shame and disgust towards the mistakes in his life. The more I read him the more I realized that, like me, he most likely let his shortcomings carry more weight than they should have, and he recognized this as a problem.

But in proper philosophical fashion, he thought about these mistakes and his humanity, battled with them, and let his reason lead him away from where his emotions were dragging him. This captured me. I've been there. I too had often attributed a substantial amount of gravity to the mistakes in my life, and I too was prone to treat most of my Christian walk like a failure. Lewis, however, seemed like he finally was on the other side of my problem. He seemed to have rationalized himself away from some of the very same conclusions I've come to about myself. He writes to a friend, "It is astonishing that sometimes we believe that we believe what, really, in our heart, we do not believe."[6] He goes on to explain that for the longest time, he claimed

6. Lewis, *Yours, Jack*, 172–73.

that he believed in the forgiveness of sins, but it never took root in his mind, until one day the truth of forgiveness became more clear than he had ever perceived it before. After years and years of confessions and going through all the religious rigmaroles that help one feel forgiven, it finally moved from his head and landed in his heart. He knew he was forgiven, but finally he was able to believe it with his whole heart.[7]

Lewis is able to proclaim and write about the power of the forgiveness of sins, while rejecting it at the same time. He claims to believe it yet is not living in it. Here, Lewis is admitting that he believes in the cross's power to forgive his mistakes, yet now he believes that he believes it! It took hold. It became practical, and no doubt changed his outlook towards God and towards himself, but it took some time to get that truth down to his heart. It took him some time and an epiphany before his emotions about his forgiveness followed his beliefs about forgiveness. *Could I reason my way out of an emotional problem?* This question excited me on an intellectual level, but more than that, on an emotional level. It was like a prisoner was handed a note from a stranger that simply said, "There's a chance you're going to get out of here soon." I did not know how. I knew little about this author, but the mere fact that there was a possibility of going back home was one that excited both the mind and the heart. So I decided to investigate this children's author a little more to see if he had anything else to offer besides the above quote and some stories about talking beavers and lions.

At first it was unintentional. I gradually began to thumb through some older C. S. Lewis books that I hadn't touched in quite some time. I occasionally found myself looking up famous quotes of his and trying to see what book those quotes were from. But then came the curiosity. It quickly became a purposeful therapeutic process. I dedicated most of my recreational reading to C. S. Lewis. I listened to lectures both about him and on his works. I took approximately three years of my life that, looking back on, I have come to call my Lewis Remedy (although I didn't know it was any type of remedy or journey at the time). I went through his signature works like *Mere Christianity, Miracles, The Screwtape Letters,* and *The Problem of Pain.* I revisited *The Chronicles of Narnia* and encountered his Space Trilogy for the first time. My devotions and Bible reading plans were Lewis-themed and -inspired. I listened to professors like Alister McGrath of Oxford give talks on Lewis and his works. During this period, I lost my older brother who served as my mentor and best friend, and Lewis's *A Grief Observed* felt like a close friend walking me through the grieving process. I read some of his biographies and his spiritual autobiography where he covered his early

7. Lewis, *Yours, Jack,* 172–73.

years and how he came to belief in God and eventually Christ. I read some compilations of his personal letters that he wrote to his friends, fans, children, and his future wife. I was even fortunate enough that, towards the end of this three-year treatment, I was able to take a C. S. Lewis class through my seminary, and study him abroad at Oxford and Cambridge where he taught, wrote, and lived. For three years or so I immersed myself in Lewis. I was much like a chronically ill man who finally found some meds that began to work: when the soothing began, I couldn't stop.

The more I read, the more the spiritual battle wounds in my soul eventually began to heal. While Lewis's writings are not Scripture and they certainly are not inerrant, if there *are* true statements about God outside of Scripture, Lewis seemed to be landing as close to those truths as any other author I've read. I found myself thinking thoughts like, *Yes, of course. I know that. Why have I never thought it or spoke it?* He put the word *suppose* in my mind: *Suppose God was like . . . Suppose this was true about God . . .*

Our souls are not meant to be beat up. They're not meant to be downcast and felt walked upon. They're meant to be uplifted. They're meant to be filled with a joy that goes beyond our ability to understand, despite our surrounding circumstances and personal mistakes. They're meant to be fulfilled by God, not kicked around and withered the way that fundamentalism, comparisons, and our own self-worth issues are happy to do for us. Life has a hopeful undertone, and our souls are supposed to reflect that, and laugh a lot along the way.

For some people, a seasoned pastor or a close friend are able to give them a hand up and out of their low self-esteem issues. For others, it may be medication that helps to balance the chemicals in their brain, and for others, it may actually be a change in their diet or exercise routine. But for me, it was "Jack" Lewis. After years of being convinced I was fumbling this whole Christianity thing, in Lewis I found a man I admired, a distant mentor I could relate to, and in Lewis I found a balm for a wounded spirit that was longing to be rehabilitated—it felt good.

As I will go on to unpack, Lewis's reason and assuredness that God accepted him, flaws and all, and his ability to communicate those beliefs so articulately did wonders for my spiritual healing. He taught me to grow up, to accept my flawed soul while still fighting to clean it up, to get over myself, to laugh more, to enjoy life more, and to, eventually, even enjoy God again. One of the greatest gifts one can give another is to show them how to simply enjoy God, with no strings attached, no memberships or conditions, and no high marks on any sort of moral scorecard, just enjoyment because he's God and he loves us. Our Creator delights in us and desires that we delight in ourselves and in him. That's a simple concept that we can really, and unnecessarily, complicate. I'll explain throughout this collection of essays which of Lewis's writings and lectures really did that for me. Maybe they may do the same for someone else.

St. Stephen's College, Oxford

I do not believe it was a coincidence that a class entitled "C. S. Lewis: Model and Mentor," taking place at Oxford and Cambridge, taught by Lewis scholar and author Robert Banks, was offered around the time I was wrapping up my own personal study of the life and works of C. S. Lewis. I had been neck-deep in Lewis theology for about three years when I saw this class as an option for my Doctor of Ministry cohort. At this point in my spiritual life, Lewis had brought me very far in my healing process. I had become emotionally involved with all of his works. So of course, I jumped on the chance to fly to Oxford and dive even deeper into the world of Narnia and all things C. S. Lewis. What a great exclamation point to put on the end of this three-year journey of healing!

After checking into my room at St. Stephen's College at Oxford, and after spending a few moments conversing with an extremely helpful and charming Oxford student named Poppy (who instantly became my friend upon walking into the building), I ventured my way down a set of stairs where I would meet my professor and all of my fellow classmates who would be experiencing the world of C. S. Lewis with me for the next several days. After shaking hands with other students representing just about every continent in the world, we opened up our laptops and the lectures began. We started off with some famous Lewis quotes, and then discussed his early life and early work before he became a believer. I was beyond excited to be there among fellow Lewis students, being taught by a published Lewis scholar, actually at Oxford where a sizable portion of the Lewis story actually played out.

I was very much relieved that I had been studying Lewis for the last several years on my own, and I did not come into this situation blind. There would have been nothing wrong with that, but the appreciation that had grown in me for this old Oxford Don made for a much more emotional and richer experience, here at this historic school. I was able to enjoy this class on a much deeper level. For me it was so much more than an academic exercise. I was meeting an old friend who had brought me farther along than I had allowed any other Christian teacher or author.

Around our first tea break our professor mentioned that one of the reasons that he picked St. Stephen's College to house us and deliver all the lectures was not only because of its geographical convenience in regards to the city of Oxford, but that it also held some historical relevance to our class's subject matter. The chapel in St. Stephen's was where Lewis used to walk to a few times a week for confession. His participation in the Anglican church encouraged his confession of trespasses to an Anglican priest . . . and I was in this building where he made those confessions. I did not waste much time. I had my fill of tea and cake. My other classmates were still chatting about, so I slipped in between a wall and my pastor friend from the Netherlands and walked out the back door of the classroom.

I made my way down some narrow halls that had been added on to and touched up over the years and through some rooms that looked like they were straight out of Hogwarts. It didn't take me long to realize that I did not know where I was going. I ended up getting lost in a labyrinth of stone hallways. I was turned all around and thought, not only may I never find the chapel, I may never find my way back to class. Perhaps these staircases were actually shifting like those in Hogwarts . . . which admittedly would have been pretty cool.

God must have seen me in my lowly condition because he sent a guide to show me the way: Poppy! In the mazes of stone hallways doubling as art exhibits I had managed to run right into my new friend. Poppy was just wonderful—one of those rare, abnormally welcoming people that you wish you could surround yourself with every day. She loved people instantly. I made a mental note that day, "Be more like Poppy." She said she would be happy to help me out.

Poppy led me down a couple flights of stairs and through a maze of stone hallways. I made a joke about how as an instructor in the Marine Corps one of my specialties was land navigation, yet here in England, I was helpless. She didn't laugh but I didn't care. She was still delightful and maintained a smile as she ushered me through her halls at Oxford. Eventually Poppy led me down the last of the ancient mazes and brought me to some stone steps that dropped down to a door that looked like it may have been the entrance to the college's dungeon, not the chapel. I thanked my guide; she gave me a hug and went on her way.

I pushed open the door to reveal a dark, surprisingly small, wooden chapel. The sun was shining through the stained-glass windows, and I could see dust particles dancing within its beams. Despite the age of this chapel, I could smell the maple and pine that made up the floor, the benches, the podium, the stage, and just about 90 percent of the entire room. It smelt like this wood was cut fresh last week. There was a Bible that had seen better days open to the book of Isaiah on the podium directly in from of me. This was still an operating chapel . . . although you could have fooled me. I was

in awe of the silence that filled the empty chapel and was torn between falling to my knees in reverence to God or pulling out a recently downloaded
"Ghost Hunting App" on my phone. I chose neither.

My boots clomped against the wooden planks on the floor and echoed
against the wall with every step I took as I slowly made my way down the
middle aisle. I took a seat on the top row in one of the chairs built into the
wall that faced the center aisle (most Anglican churches are built in this
fashion). Across the room were two more rows of built-in chairs that faced
me. I imagined myself in this wooden chair that made me sit much more
upright than I was accustomed to, sitting during an actual liturgy. I know
I wouldn't have lasted long in that service, not with the comfy chairs I had
grown accustomed to in my home churches. My passion for God in the
moment would have had to outweigh the discomfort of those center-facing
oak chairs. Most of my attention would have been focused on not trying
to make eye contact with my counterpart sitting directly across from me.
Everyone could see me scrolling on my phone during this church service. I sat
there, upright, for about ten minutes.

I thumbed through the *English Book of Common Prayer* briefly before
placing it back under my chair and breathing in the chapel again. This was
where Lewis came for confession. This was the room where Lewis dealt with
the idea of forgiveness and redemption in real time. Here I was, spending
the last few years trying to convince my heart of what my head claimed to
believe: that God is good, that his forgiveness is real, consistent, and thor-
ough, and here I was in the very room where the man who helped me get
there used to come to ask for forgiveness of his mistakes.

Lewis writes in a letter, "I think that if God forgives us we must forgive
ourselves. Otherwise it is almost like setting up ourselves as a higher tribu-
nal than Him."[8] I had that line memorized as it was one of the rational tools
Lewis had given me to combat my emotions that were fighting against my
reason. God forgives us but we cannot forgive ourselves? Are we better than
God? Do we know more about ourselves than *he* does? Our Creator says
"redeemed," while we have the blatant nerve to say "condemned"? *Who the
heck are we?* What a tremendously powerful thought to carry in one's back
pocket. What freedom I found in that one statement alone. *Was this the
room where Lewis first contemplated that thought?*

It was a brief yet emotional experience for me. I used that time to get
down on my knees and thank God for how far I had come in my journey
with him, how different I had come to see him now, and to confess a few of
the mistakes I had in the back of my mind . . . it felt good.

8. Lewis, *Letters of C. S. Lewis*, 523.

It wasn't long, however, before my humanity kicked in and I thought about someone walking in on me, kneeling in an empty, dark chapel by myself, and thought about how unsettling that would be for them and, curiously, how embarrassing it would have been for me. So, I finished the prayer, dusted off my kneecaps, and made my way back to our classroom, without the assistance of my friend Poppy, having never tested out my Ghost Hunting App . . . *next time.*

There will be topics discussed in this book that explain why Lewis was such a help to people like myself, but it may be beneficial to discuss one right from the beginning, sort of like a pretreatment.

If the reader is not familiar with Lewis, it's important to know that he had an uncanny knack for looking at things differently. He had an uncanny knack for writing things we did not know we agreed with until we heard them. He had an uncanny knack for taking preconceived ideas that we have grown up to see as a negative and turning them into a positive. What was once a liability that we hide from the general public, Lewis is able to flip upside-down and turn into an asset that we use to remind ourselves about God's continuing progress in our story. Case in point: evil.

For someone like me, the sensation of feeling evil is easy to inhabit. We may not call it evil. That may be too strong for our modern sensibilities. We may simply call it feeling bad or feeling ugly inside. We might say we're flawed or erroneous. But whatever we call it, it is the opposite of good. So, for the sake of argument, let's just call it evil.

The cycle happens too regularly: we make a mistake, we feel bad, and whether or not we apologize for it and whether or not we are forgiven, we always walk away kind of thinking that there is something uniquely wrong with us. We're different. Other people do not do what we do. Other people are good. We're bad. We're dark. If anyone knew the real us, they'd be appalled. We're evil.

I've always known about the cross and its power to forgive all mistakes: past, present, and future. I knew all about why Christ was the perfect substitute for our mistakes. I can even help others understand this. But telling my heart that it was not evil in spite of all that was a difficult task. I learned to accept that I was just spiritually inept and prone to gaffes, and God would have to deal with me one day.

Do not get me wrong. If there is high-handed disobedience in my life that I am aware of, then that *should* bring about negative feelings that would lead me to the cross and to others for forgiveness. But beyond that, walking around feeling like some kind of less-than follower of Christ because of my proclivity to make mistakes is simply something from hell. Feeling evil has no place in our lives. I knew that cognitively, but I could not embrace it emotionally. Lewis helped me mend that 18-inch gap between my head and my heart by thinking about the very nature of evil.

Lewis would say that the actions that made me feel evil were not in fact evil. They were something else entirely. They certainly weren't positive. They certainly weren't something that would enhance my life. They were merely what he called spoiled goodness.

Lewis writes in one of his signature books, *Mere Christianity*, "Wickedness, when you examine it, turns out to be the pursuit of some good in the wrong way."[9] All of our mistakes are actually the pursuit of something good. He goes on to explain that we can be good, for the simple sake of doing a good act, but we cannot be bad for the simple sake of being bad. We may do something nice for someone just because it is the right thing to do, even if we do not feel like doing it. We will, however, never do something cruel to somebody simply because it was the wrong thing to do. No one does a cruel act merely for the sake of the cruel act because cruelty, at face value, is not useful.[10] It's all an attempt at something greater.

Everything we've attempted, no matter how wonderful or deplorable, is an attempt at restitution. It's an attempt at wholeness and oneness. Even the most heinous and cruel acts are what Lewis would call a "misguided attempt at redemption" (that phrase will be discussed later in the book.)

We are a creation that has been separated from its Creator, and although we may not recognize it, we feel it . . . and we do not like it. So we take these blind shots in the dark, hoping to mend that gap. Some try to mend it by stealing whatever it is that they think will fill that void, others try to mend it by giving to the poor. Some try to mend it by being a bully and demeaning those around them, others try to mend it by avoiding conflict their whole lives. Some try to feel whole by addictively turning to harmful substances, others try to fill it by health and wellness. Some try to mend the gap between them and redemption through a career, others try to mend it by organized religion. Some people put the weight of their soul on their spouse or significant other, others put the weight of their soul on a church, or the staff that run it.

While it is important for someone's offense to be recognized as just that, an offense in need of cleansing (and sometimes punishment), it is also

9. Lewis, *Mere Christianity*, 44.
10. Lewis, *Mere Christianity*, 44.

helpful to know why we have the capacity for doing evil acts. Is it because we are in fact evil people? Or are we desperately trying to redeem ourselves with whatever we think will fill that void, no matter how holy or ungodly our methods of trying to do so? The point is that a mistake does not make us a bad person, nor does a lifetime of mistakes. A "criminal" is not in fact a criminal. A "criminal" is a person who has crime in their past. There's a difference. A human being does not have the capability to take on a single label because of one act (or several acts) of badness. Mankind does not have the capability to be bad for the mere sake of being bad. Lewis continues:

> In other words, badness cannot succeed even in being bad in the same way in which goodness is good. *Goodness is, so to speak, itself: badness is only spoiled goodness.* And there must be something good first before it can be spoiled.[11]

Lewis would say that evil is not a proactive force. It does not really exist. It is simply this spoiled goodness.[12] It is what is left when all goodness has been drained out of something. Goodness was here first, and evil is only making a temporary show of things where goodness has left. As Aslan the Great Lion explained to the Sons of Adam and the Daughters of Eve, "though the Witch knew the Deep Magic, there is a magic deeper still which she did not know." Her knowledge went back "only to the dawn of Time,"[13] which is a created thing; but because nature has all the air of a good thing spoiled,[14] and because Christ is the beginning and the end, we were never meant to be evil: God never created an evil world, and any evil in the world will one day be eradicated. The Christian can take some solace that this problem of evil is but a blip on the radar in the grand existence that is us, a blip that is floating farther and farther away as I write this.

Not to get too theological too soon, but this is why it is important in the biblical account that Satan is a fallen angel, not an equal but opposite created evil force. Goodness was here long before evil, and goodness will be here long afterwards. Lewis writes that if good is the tree, then evil is the ivy.[15] Ivy cannot grow on its own. It must attach itself to something else for support. The ivy is dependent on the tree. Evil is dependent on goodness. If evil and goodness were both of equal substance and equal power, there would not be a right and a wrong. It would simply be left to a matter of

---

11. Lewis, *Mere Christianity*, 44.
12. Lewis, *Mere Christianity*, 35.
13. Lewis, *Lion, Witch*, 132.
14. Lewis, *Miracles*, 196.
15. Lewis, "Evil and God," 5.

preference. Lewis writes in an essay called "Evil and God," most often found today in a collection called *God in the Dock*, "If evil has the same kind of reality as good, the same autonomy and completeness, our allegiance to good becomes the arbitrarily chosen loyalty of a partisan."[16] We have to know of goodness before we recognize badness. One has to rule over the other for us to differentiate. As Lewis points out in this essay, sane men understand lunacy because they know what sanity looks like. This should be good news because the only reason we see the darkness inside of us is because we are, in all actuality, good people. When we cling to goodness we cling to the real and the eternal. When we cling to badness, we're clinging to a temporary parasite that will be extinguished one great day. The badness that we choose is much smaller and much more insignificant than the goodness inside. One is just hitching a ride like a flea on a dog. One day goodness will scratch it off.

Our most futile mistakes all the way down to the most horrendous of crimes means that we have spoiled goodness in us, but we ourselves are not bad. We are not bad people in the way we often feel as such. We are good people. We are good people who long to be made whole and feel redeemed. Yet we have this spoiled goodness in us, and it is going to rear its ugly head in big ways and in small ways, from now until the only One who can redeem us un-spoils the goodness that's been so infected by our humanity.

Christians like me, who feel that they are generally a bad person because of their ability to choose the wrong path, should be comforted to know that they are not walking, talking evil people. There is simply a lack of goodness in certain areas of their lives. Yes, we are prone to do some awful things. We are desperately in need of redemption and will naturally flow towards the dark side if we're not proactively turning towards the light, but the default human heart was good and longed for God from the beginning, and that's the heart that will return to humanity once evil is shown the back door.

The good news is that where there is a lack of something, something can always be put there. A sad view of Christianity is one that is made up of simply keeping the bad stuff out and not putting the good stuff in. Evil has nowhere to move in when goodness has taken up residency. Filling one's life with the things of God, whatever that means to the individual Christian, is a good way to begin not feeling like an evil person.

When I felt evil in my life, it was because my life was missing something good, not because I was something evil. If two dogs are going to fight and one has been given a lot to eat while the other has been denied food

16. Lewis, "Evil and God," 5.

for a period of time, the well-fed dog will win every time (even if that dog is a temporary, evil dog, dependent on the good dog for his existence). A big part of my healing was learning that Christianity was much more than trying to deny myself evil desires but filling my life with goodness. Where there was evil, it was simply a lack of goodness. I have to proactively fill the gaps with goodness and allow that to be my focus.

Lewis's turning my idea of evil upside down is just one of several examples of how his books, lectures, essays, poems, and jokes changed my heart and helped me fall back in love with God. As this book progresses, and my journey with Lewis unfolds, I will discuss many more ideas that should be helpful for any follower of Christ.

I have a son. Often, while his room is still dirty, while there is filth under his fingernails and his hair is in need of a deep cleansing, I still take great joy in him . . . just by his presence. I would equally expect him to be comforted by the fact that his father delights in him as a dirty little boy (whom I love). I want him to feel secure in this. I am not routinely worried about the filth because I know the bathtub awaits him. My concern is that he feels valued by the fact that his daddy loves him and treasures him more than he could possibly know. I know about the dirt. I'm going to take care of the dirt . . . but for now let's move forward with simply enjoying each other. *Why do I think my relationship with my Heavenly Father should be any different?* That's a logical thought that should be able to bleed into my emotions.

Our souls thirst for this kind of enjoyment. Indeed, it makes sense why they do. They were created to be sustained by it, the way our physical bodies were created to be sustained by food and water. When our souls are denied enjoying God, our souls dry up. They become bitter and angry, either hating God or hating themselves . . . or both. So before I cover some of Lewis's works that impacted me the most, and helped me enjoy God again, let me paint a better picture of the spiritual condition I was in when I met C. S. Lewis. Maybe someone reading will relate.

2

Low Spiritual Self-Esteem

My idea of God is a not divine idea. It has to be shattered from time to time. He shatters it Himself. He is the great iconoclast. Could we not almost say that this shattering is one of the marks of His presence?

—C. S. Lewis, *A Grief Observed*[1]

I F having one's view of God shattered is one of the marks of his presence, I can assuredly say that my three years immersed in the Lewis Remedy were vital in reintroducing God's presence back into my life. In the early parts of my Christian journey, my reoccurring lessons about all the ways that God was upset with me, while leaving out the parts about the cross that removed that wrath, planted the seed of a spiritual condition that I've had to contend with for most of my Christian life. I can't point to any one individual pastor or church leader who would preach God's anger towards my non-spiritual perfection, but it was in the air. It snuck its way into the pulpit, youth camps, Sunday school lessons, and Christian radio and television. Growing up in the Midwest, engulfed in our Christian culture, our camps and conferences, our Christian clubs at school, our radio stations, our Christian stores, and even our Christian t-shirts that played off slogans of popular brands . . . all of these served as a constant reminder that I was just not very good at being a Christian.

I simply was not good at our Christian culture. I struggled to be a player within it. I'm not necessarily anti these things, just someone who

---

1. Lewis, *Grief Observed*, 66.

never felt like he belonged in the midst of them. A young person who grows up with chronic self-worth issues surrounded by fundamentalist religion is not a good recipe for a flourishing relationship with his or her Creator.

Take music for example. It's a trivial example I know, and it does not seem to be an issue today, thank God, but perhaps it will assist me in painting a better picture of my "less-than" spiritual condition.

I was very much into all sorts of music growing up. I went through a country music phase, classic rock and roll, and dabbled in rap and R&B. But the genre that seemed to stick and resonate with me the most was punk rock. I loved it. It spoke my language and spoke it very loudly and quickly. I listened to all sorts of punk. I listened to underground punk, mainstream, pop punk, skater, Celtic, ska, it didn't matter. I had favorite bands representing all facets. Yet, punk rock was generally not accepted within our mainstream Christian culture at the time. Christians had their versions of punk rock, and I sincerely tried to like them, but I just did not find them to be as good—lyrically, musically, or in performance. So I listened to mostly non-Christian bands. I did not recognize them as non-Christian. I just simply recognized them as bands that I enjoyed. I didn't know I was bucking any sort of acceptable Christian cultural norms. I apparently was, however. "Non-Christian music is bad for your soul," I was often reminded. This was a fact that was grilled into me during my early adolescence and teenage years. I remember in church, a pastor asked us that if we would not put a small piece of poop in cookie batter and eat it afterwards, why would we ingest a small piece of bad music into our soul?

I remember once telling my lunch table how much fun I had in the mosh pit at a punk rock show I had been to recently in Dallas, and the girl that I had a crush on at the time scolded me for going to such a "dark place." This of course made me feel really bad . . . mostly because she was very attractive, but also because at that time I believed her.

I recall a poster in a Christian book store that had a list of secular bands on the left and their Christian counterparts on the right. The bands on the left were sure to make us engage in premarital sex and booze while the bands on the right sang about one topic and one topic only: God. I remember thinking, *but I have so much more going on in my life!* A lot of songs I listen to did glorify God, but a lot of the music that resonated with me had to do with my school struggles, girl problems, and teenage politics in general. *Why can't I listen to music that encompasses all of me, not just one element? . . . albeit the most important.* And on top of that, the Christian counterparts to these bands were not apt comparisons. (*Was dc Talk really the best counterpart to Green Day?*) . . . I was suspicious of that poster.

Regardless, at one point my fellow youth-groupers and I eventually made the decision to *only* listen to "Christian" music—that is, whatever albums were being sold in the religious sections at the department store. The local department stores were now in charge of choosing which music would edify my soul and which would not. Nevertheless, I got rid of all of my non-Christian music and felt slightly more righteous than I was before. God must have been quite impressed. I had followed the example of my fellow midwestern contemporaries and partook in a musical diet of Christian culture's Top 40.

I am aware that there may be some people who cannot handle listening to music that sometimes counteracts what they believe. Maybe it really does drag them into unhealthy situations, enhance an addiction, or cause them to disrespect women. Some may need the self-imposed rule of "Christian music only," and that's fine. It may be a very healthy way to connect with God. For me it didn't work. We are all individuals, with different personalities, who all connect with God in different ways, and that is something to be celebrated. Not broken down and conformed.

So naturally, my Christian-music-only diet did not last long. I missed my music. I missed my bands. I started quietly buying all my favorite albums again and began enjoying my favorite bands. Soon I began to fill my head with their power-chords riffs, melodic choruses, and lyrics about girls, fights, skating, and parties. Yet, I couldn't help but notice all my counterparts still listening to the mainstream Christian Top 40. I felt off. I felt different. I wondered why they were fine listening to the same popular stuff over and over again and why I desired something different. I really tried to force it. I really tried to make myself conform. But I couldn't. I started feeling there was something wrong with me spiritually. Was I not as motivated about God as much as they were? Did I not love God the same way? Was my nonconformance a sign that I was a less-than Christian? It sure began to feel like it.

Again, music is a trite example I know. I do not look back on the youth pastors or fellow youth groupers who encouraged this secular purge with any sort of negative feelings. But this was just one example out of many times that I felt that, because I wasn't conforming to the religious culture around me, I wasn't what God was looking for. I began to feel like I didn't love God as much as those other Christians . . . the ones that don't mosh . . . the ones who don't go to Rated R movies . . . the ones who proudly wore WWJD on their wrist, when my bracelet said the name of whatever punk show I was most recently at. This is a picture of a midwestern kid who loved Jesus and wanted to wholeheartedly please God yet struggled to feel comfortable in the youth-group crowd. I felt like a Christian, but not one as excited about Jesus as the guy next to me. I felt like someone that couldn't cut it in mainstream, God-pleasing Christianity. I put God into the box of midwestern Christian culture, and if I wasn't excited about that, I wasn't excited about God. Plus, I had no interest in volleyball, and that will quickly isolate a midwestern Christian teenager just as quickly as anything else.

There are other examples that made me feel isolated. We were encouraged to surround ourselves with Christians friends only. Yet I had friends who were not believers. I did not feel that I should stay away from them in the way I was encouraged to do (that actually seemed the opposite of what I should be doing.) The country bonfires after football games seemed more enticing to me than the local Baptist Church's "5th Quarter." I liked trick-or-treating a bit more than the trunk-or-treating in the Methodist Church's parking lot. After prom, I wanted to go to the lake with my friends rather than play bingo and eat pizza in the new Family Life Center at the church.

These Christian-themed events weren't bad, in fact, I saw them as a positive in our community. Looking back, they probably would have set me up for spiritual success much more than the decisions I made. Yet, I saw this struggle and this nonconformity as a constant reminder of me being on the outside of the widely accepted views of what a Christian should be participating in, who he should be hanging out with, and what he should be listening too. I looked at my friend Scott, who is still a dear friend. Scott had this midwestern Christianity thing down pat. He was Mr. Youth Group. He was the head of our Fellowship of Christian Athletes. He played bass in our town's First Baptist Church. He wore the shirt of the latest Christian band to come through town. His purity ring never left his ring finger. He only dated one girl his entire life, and they didn't even kiss until their wedding day (at least I assumed at the time). His hair was perfectly spiked with bleached blond tips that stretched gloriously up towards the God that he served. He was what God-pleasing spirituality looked like. Not me. I was different. I was weird. I was on the outside.

Enter the condition: this less-than feeling that started taking root as a wannabe-Christ-following teenager saw how he *should* be living—a prominent participator in our culture's Christian activities—but saw what he *really* desired—pretty much anything but. I started developing this condition as a teenager and I would take it with me long into adulthood . . . even into professional ministry.

It is a condition that has been so forceful and present in my life that I have even given it a name, much like a medical condition that just will not go away. I have diagnosed this condition: low spiritual self-esteem. I will define low spiritual self-esteem as the following: *the perpetual feeling that, while I know God does love me, my failures and shortcomings (past, present, and future) cause him to see me as just a little less than others who do not seem to struggle in the ways that I do.* His plans for me are less. His expectations are low. His pride in me? Even lower.

In Lewis's *The Chronicles of Narnia: Prince Caspian*, after encountering Aslan the Great Lion for the first time in a while, Lucy throws her little arms around his neck, buries her face in his great mane and exclaims:

> "Aslan," said Lucy, "you're bigger."
>> "That is because you are older, little one," answered he.
>> "Not because you are?"
>> "I am not. But every year you grow, you will find me bigger."[2]

". . . every year you grow, you will find me bigger."

How many of us develop an elementary view of God that we were taught as a child or adolescent and cling to it for the rest of our lives? Many, I suppose. What a disservice to the gospel. My view of God was very elementary, and it had to be expanded. It must constantly be shattered and rebuilt, stronger and fuller. It must grow. Let me try to illustrate what low spiritual self-esteem looks like.

I was not the best basketball player in middle school; in fact, I was awful. I was a little chubby, a little shorter than the other kids, and I had zero coordination when it came to running and dribbling. Unless we were winning or losing by a couple dozen, I did not see much court time. When I *did* get to play, Coach played me because he had to, not because he was proud to do so.

"Braudrick hasn't played in the last three games, we're losing by thirty-eight, guess I should toss him in there."

I have a strong memory of falling flat on my face, unprovoked, in the middle of the court at an away game, tripping over my grandpa's hand-me-down Reeboks. (I wasn't my coach's secret weapon to say the least.)

Yet, I liked my coach. He was funny, young, and popular with all the students. Some of the girls had a crush on him. I liked him, and generally wanted him to like me too. But I saw the way he interacted and treated his first-string players, and I saw the way he interacted with and treated me. There was a distinct difference. They were his prized jewels, his key to winning. I was a name on his roster.

---

2. Lewis, *Prince Caspian*, 141.

I knew my place. I knew I would never be a first-string player. Despite my daydreams of hitting the game-winning shot when I practiced on my goal at home, I would never earn my coach's acceptance and friendship through my basketball skills. I had to accept my place as third-string player . . . and I did.

Today this bothers me very little. I never go to bed at night and wonder what my basketball coach from middle school thinks of me, nor do I have any desires or dreams of basketball glory. (I never did much recover from my height disadvantage, but I've come to terms with that as well.) Unfortunately, my view of God took this very same merit-based direction when I first started realizing the darkness that existed in my life. I realized that I knew right from wrong, but somehow had the proclivity to choose the wrong. I didn't like it. I projected this view of my basketball coach onto God: if I do good, God loves me and is proud to have me on the team; if I do bad, I am an embarrassment that needs to stay benched. My view of God had morphed into a middle school mindset and had remained there for years. It needed to grow.

This condition stuck with me throughout my early twenties as well. I wanted to follow Christ and wanted to be good Christian (though I am not sure what the term good Christian means now), however, I ended up suffering many soul-wounding setbacks on my journey to becoming a "good Christian." Despite my longings to maintain a strong Christian walk, I had several relationship failures, including an early divorce. I had several bouts with alcohol, mostly throughout my time in the Marine Corps, and struggled with many overall negative habits that people do not associate with being a good Christian. I became a single dad while I was studying and preparing to be in a profession that places high value on strong families. I could go on . . .

I loved Jesus though. I loved him through it all—I never stopped. He made sense to me. I felt broken often, but I felt like Jesus had a heart for broken people, despite how I acted in my brokenness. Although I struggled to accept his forgiveness and restoration, I kept coming back to him. I don't know why. I assumed he was very disappointed.

It was during these periods of staunch brokenness that I learned to love the people he loved. I fell in love with broken people like me. I became very attracted to people who struggled with finding their place in life, and not just for ministry purposes. When broken people are the recipients of a minister's ministry, but not the recipients of their daily friendship, there is very little ministering taking place.

This heart for the marginalized in our society made me want a better platform to engage them. So, I went to seminary after the Marines because, well, I guess I just thought I was supposed to. I eventually went into professional ministry because I felt a draw and passion for the "least of these."[3] I began organizing events that mobilized people in my church to get involved serving the poor in our community. I started a prison nonprofit ministry that supported the church behind prison walls. I eventually was honored to direct a community outreach center focused on community development in the inner-cities of Oklahoma City that my church was courageous enough to launch. Although that whole time I was still struggling with my standing before God, I was drawn towards ministry. C. S. Lewis had not finished his work with me when I decided to jump in the trenches of serving others. I don't believe any Christian should wait until they have cleaned themselves up sufficiently before they get off the sidelines and serve others. If that was the case, they would remain benched for life. So, despite my shortcomings, I served God by serving others, the best I knew how, all while battling the blitzkrieg assault that was my low spiritual self-esteem.

A professor in seminary once told me that because of my divorce, I was, and I quote, "disqualified from professional ministry." That did not help. I was already aware that I was not measuring up. I was already deeply ashamed of my divorce. Now I was wasting my life, chasing a calling that I was unqualified to chase . . . low spiritual self-esteem.

For the longest time, this was the reflection in the mirror. This was the progress report I so often held up when comparing myself to the seemingly spiritual giants at church and at work around me. How could God possibly find use for me when he has so many other first-stringers to put in the game? This tattooed, divorced Marine was on the lower end of the spiritual totem pole. God was a coach who had to accept me on the team because that was his character, but he was in no way beaming with pride to do so . . . not over this third-stringer who could not seem to shake these pesky shortcomings. I was, as Lewis would describe, a muddy and tattered child.[4]

What an embarrassingly pathetic view of God I carried around with me for so long. God be praised, it did not last.

3. Matt 25:40.
4. Lewis, *Letters of C. S. Lewis*, 470.

While this book will delve into some of the roots causes of low spiritual self-esteem that Lewis helped me to uncover, and of course some remedies and maintenance strategies, it is important to discuss at this point, the desire to change. If anyone is ever going to benefit from reading and applying Lewis, reading and applying Scripture, or really going on any sort of self-betterment adventure, there has to be an actual desire there. Sometimes we can agree that we need to change, but we do not desire it. There's a big difference. Many of the causes of my low spiritual self-esteem came from knowing there were areas of my life that needed fixing, but deep down not really wanting to fix them.

Lewis writes in *Mere Christianity*, "Before we can be cured, we must want to be cured. Those who really wish for help will get it."[5] As a Christian, the obvious answer to the question "Do we want to be cured?" is a resounding "Yes," but that may not always play out practically. Lewis writes, "A famous Christian long ago told us that when he was a young man he prayed constantly for chastity; but years later he realized that while his lips had been saying 'Oh Lord, make me chaste,' his heart had been secretly adding, 'But please don't do it just yet.'"[6] When the inevitable failure comes, and we bring our mistakes quickly to God, we should ask ourselves, *Do I actually want to be cured? Or am I just going through my religious motions?* Do we truly want surrender? Or do we just not want to feel bad anymore? When we pray "Forgive us our trespasses, as we have forgiven those who trespass against us,"[7] do we attach real, garment-tearing remorse and a deep desire to do better next time, or is it just some magical words to clear our palette? There has to be some desire to change, even if it is the smallest, most minute desire we've ever had; we need to align our heads and our heart in agreement that, not only do we need to change, we want to as well.

Being repulsed by my low spiritual self-esteem was a necessary ingredient. Having a small view of God was a necessary ingredient as well. One has to actually, at the deepest level of their core, desire to change. I had to truly desire that my view of God grow, not keep him in a comfortable box that I could understand. This had to be developed before I dove into my Lewis Remedy. The posture of my heart needed to change. I needed to want something to be different, not simply agree that it needed to be different. I had to ask myself the tough questions—not in a way that brought guilt, in a

5. Lewis, *Mere Christianity*, 99.

6. Lewis, *Mere Christianity*, 99.

7. Matt 6:14.

way that brought change. I had to let myself be disgusted with the fact that I was devouring mere mud pies instead of basking in the beautiful relationship with God I could have. That, even the smallest version of that, is the only way to allow real change to occur.

If one takes C. S. Lewis seriously, he demands that their view of God grow. He helped expand my view of God in ways others probably should have, but for whatever reasons failed to do so . . . or I failed to let them. Maybe Lewis's children's stories slipped a view of God past my guard that I was not expecting and normally would reject, or maybe it was the way he was able to articulate so perfectly what my mind was longing to piece together and knew to be true, yet could not articulate. It was as if I had this murky soup floating around in my mind and Lewis was able to draw out the exact recipe, put it in order, and make it make sense. Whatever the reason, the spiritual healing it brought was long overdue. I was clinging to my middle-school, stained-glass view of God for too long, and it was painful. So when Lewis came along, I was happy to give him the shattering hammer.

There is so much more freedom and so much more beauty found in expanding one's view of God. My view of God had to grow, and it must continue to do so. It must be shattered and rebuilt. So early on in the Lewis Remedy, I made up my mind to let my view of God expand. I told myself, *here is a guy that I have connected with for some reason or another; most of the other teachers in my past have not gotten me very far, so I am going to clear out all of my presuppositions and give God a new platform to speak to me.* In my morning Scripture reading I made it a point to not view my reading through what I had been told before; instead I would give God a clean slate to speak to my soul. I asked myself new questions. I asked, *if this is true, if Christ really said this, and if I truly believe this is God's word, what does that mean for me today, as I sit here a depraved man dependent on grace?* I dove into what became a three-year journey, determined to let my view of God expand to new levels, desperate to fall back in love with someone I had developed a dislike for because of his assumed dislike for me. Needless to say, years later, I made progress. Book after book, essay after essay, lecture after lecture, the calluses began to fall off. My prayers were intentional. I asked God for a new passion. I begged God to allow my mind to expand and to have but a germ of desire for him . . . the real him. After encountering Lewis the way that I did—studying his life and reading his words over this period of three years—my view of God expanded to liberating proportions.

For people who know that their diet is having undesirable outcomes, such as allergic reactions or chronic nausea, but they are unsure which food is to blame, there's a procedure called an Elimination Diet. An Elimination Diet is a process of a nutritionist helping a client isolate his or her nutritional problems by eliminating all of a certain type of food and then, one at a time, reintroducing selected foods back into their diet. They keep this process going until a certain food causes the familiar negative reaction. Now they know which food is to blame. The client could have walked around for years with allergic reactions or nausea, having never known the root cause until someone from the outside helped identify the problem. They may have been treating the rashes on their skin with topical ointment for years before they knew it was actually tree nuts or soy. The same thing happens in both the psychological realms and the spiritual.

Far too often we carry around weight that we do not even know we are carrying. The surface level emotions that we are in a constant battle with are rarely the issue itself. They are a symptom of what lies beneath. Often, we are not emotionally mature enough to connect the dots down below and articulate the root causes of our problems. We need someone to step in and do it for us. I used to go to a professional counselor named Ben. He was masterful at connecting people's emotions with their past and connecting their current feelings to their fears, hopes, their personality, and even poor diets. Ben was a huge help. I think we all need a Ben in our life. Going to professional counseling is not a sign that we are weak. It is a sign that we are intentional. But, the purpose of this book is to explain how C. S. Lewis helped me. Ben deserves his own book.

Before discussing some of the ways that Lewis helped expand my view of God, and thus brought a degree of healing to my low spiritual self-esteem, it may be beneficial to diagnose some deeper causes of my condition, causes that were not surface level until Lewis brought them into the light. Perhaps the reader has experienced one or two of these causes.

PART 2

Essays on the Causes

3

Dabbling in the Shallow

You never know how much you really believe anything until its truth or false-hood becomes a matter of life and death to you.

—C. S. Lewis, *A Grief Observed*[1]

I LOVE the above line from Lewis's *A Grief Observed*. Lewis goes on to use the example of a rope. It is easy for one to say that he believes in the strength of a rope to keep a mailed package together without ever actually testing it. But if the same man wants to bungee jump off a cliff, he may want to make sure the rope has been given a solid test or two. The matter of the rope is now one of life and death.

I saw this example while serving in the Marine Corps Infantry. All throughout our training we were taught about cover and concealment. It's pretty simple really. Concealment hides you from your enemy's sight. Cover hides you from your enemy's bullets. In an actual firefight it's preferred to have both. But, as is the case with many things, the value of cover and concealment is not fully appreciated until it is tested. Early on in my eight-year Marine Corps career, we would train with blanks. All that means is the bullets that we would put into our magazine and then into our M-16s were explosive, but they would send no projectile out of the barrel. They would make a large "pop" sound, but the fake enemy in front of you was never in real harm. Cover and concealment were important in training, but if the projectiles weren't actually coming down range, they were simply a training commodity. Sometimes simply kneeling behind a bush would suffice.

1. Lewis, *A Greif Observed*, 22–23.

29

I remember once however, when we went to a simulation course. It was basically a bunch of cinderblock buildings made up to resemble a Middle Eastern village. The core of our M-16s were replaced to be able to house non-lethal simulation rounds. For once we were finally able to experience what is was like to be shot at, as rounds rained down on us in the form of a 9mm bullet with a hard, plastic tip on it. These would explode upon contact, leaving behind a paint stain and an awful, painful welt or bruise. These were not paint balls. These got your attention when they struck.

The first time I was hit with a paint simulation round I took cover and concealment a lot more seriously. It hurt. I was not content to hide behind a bush anymore the way I did when the opposing team simply fired blanks at me. I needed concrete. When paint rounds came down range, I had more of a vested interest in taking cover and concealment a bit more seriously. Then, of course, when we went to combat it became a matter of life and death. Our ability to find cover and concealment was exposed the moment it became painful not to have it. Our skills and preparation were tested the moment we came under fire. The bushes no longer did anything for us, and one hopes they didn't grow dependent on them in training. The same is true in our day-to-day life. When turmoil hits, the seriousness one takes their faith becomes evident. It is exposed as a weak bush or a strong concrete wall, but it is exposed regardless. Sometimes that exposure is jarring.

When Lewis wrote the above line, it was in a moment when his faith was exposed by the death of his wife. Before his faith was tested in such a jarring way, it could have easily just been a cultural commodity. But now it had entered the proving grounds. Was his faith an acceptable, easygoing addition to his social life? Or was it able to sustain him while he was being fired upon by the enemy?

We Western Christians often never have the spiritual luxury of having our faith tested. We never are faced with the choice of complete surrender to God or lose everything we value, including our lives. We may never have the privilege of asking God for literal daily bread. We can get along in our culture quite well without the truth or falsehood of our faith in Christ ever being exposed.

I remember seeing a recording of a Christian church in Mosel, Iraq while it was under ISIS control. This was during a time when members of ISIS were literally crucifying Christians. A church that used to meet freely and worship openly was now forced to do so in the most secret of circumstances. They were in a darkened room with no light, no air, and no source of Scripture. Yet what were they doing? They were singing "Lord I Lift Your Name on High" in Arabic. Hands were raised. Tears were falling. If a member of ISIS would have discovered them, it would have been a death sentence to them and their whole families—most likely a very agonizing death at that. Many of them had the opportunity to leave town on a ransom, but they stayed. Many of them had the opportunity to join ISIS, but they refused. They kept their church together during the most trying times of their existence.

I remember watching that footage and not only feeling very emotional but feeling very small. These men, women, and children were giants of the faith. Their surrender to God was on full display. They were tested and were passing the test with flying colors. They would be one of the unknown glorious ones in heaven one day, that we would all be clamoring to ask what they did. They were larger than I. They were in full surrender.

I am a living example that it is possible to have one foot in full surrender to God and have the other one fighting to step in the opposite direction . . . saying I trust Christ, but letting my life and actions prove otherwise. Despite being a Christian, I have had the ongoing and annoying tendency of being afraid to give up the areas of my life that bring me comfort, no matter how much I know God wants me to let go of them. Apparently, Lewis struggled with this too. In "A Slip of the Tongue," one of my favorite essays Lewis ever wrote (which today is most often found in the compilation *The Weight of Glory*), he writes:

> This is my endlessly recurrent temptation: to go down to that Sea (I think St. John of the Cross called God a Sea) and there neither dive nor swim nor float, but only dabble and splash, careful not to get out of my depth and holding on to the lifeline which connects me with my things temporal.[2]

This could be my life's summary statement for the majority of my relationship with God. Like many Christians, I enjoy the things of God. I have learned how to get along in the church world alright: the kids' programs; the youth group trips; the singles' functions; even earning a paycheck in professional ministry. My life indeed has been better having been a part of my country's Christian culture. But dabbling in the sea which is God? Enjoying the splashing on my face and the coolness on my feet, while also holding on to the edge? Afraid of letting go in full surrender and trust? This has been the picture. The temporal in my life has been given way too much attention and emotional weight. Relationships, careers, finance—all of these

2. Lewis, "A Slip," 187.

I can recall examples of me stressing, taking the reins, and doing things my way instead of God's . . . again, again, and again. This has been my "endlessly recurrent temptation." I am happy to hand God the steering wheel of my life, only to grab it back when we go off-roading.

Lewis, however, reminded me that true joy comes from total abandonment to God. Lewis writes, "Our whole being by its very nature is one vast need; incomplete, preparatory, empty yet cluttered, crying out for Him,"[3] and without handing over complete trust to God, our loose ends will never be tied. My soul will continue to cry out no matter how many times I was in church that month. Lewis says that I must not hold on to even the smallest ounce of hell.[4] He reminded me that in order to have the best relationship with my Creator I can have, and hence, be more fulfilled than I currently am, I must give everything to God, giving him the reins when I would rather hold them tight to my chest, trusting him with the results. Lewis proclaimed, "He claims all, because He is love and must bless. He cannot bless us unless he has us. When we try to keep within us an area that is our own, we try to keep an area of death. Therefore in love, he claims all."[5] In my most honest moments, there have been many times I'd prefer to cling to my chest instead of give to God—a lack of trust.

Lewis's ability to enjoy the immediate things of God while still clinging to the temporal is something any honest Christian should be able to relate to. I know I do. *I know that I should be more giving with my time, money, and resources now, but I've just got too much going on right now . . . I prefer to hold on to the temporal; I know I should take a moment to pray and read Scripture to my son tonight, but it has been a long day and I gave my coworkers all of my energy . . . I prefer to hold on to the temporal; I know my dating life has been an utter disaster, but instead of holding out until I am spiritually and relationally healthy, I'll just jump to the next in line . . . I prefer to hold on to the temporal; I know I should forgive . . . but I choose to hold on to the temporal; I know I'm pushing my personal boundaries . . . but I choose to hold on to the temporal; I know I should treat those with whom I disagree with love and respect . . . but I choose to hold on to the temporal.*

Fill in the blank with any one of the several reoccurring mistakes I've allowed to remain in my life: pride, alcohol, wasting my resources, unforgiveness, self-centeredness, living for religion more than I was living for Christ. I've pushed the boundaries in all of these areas, flirting with disaster (though many times I've completely catapulted over those boundaries),

---

3. Lewis, *Four Loves*, 4.

4. Lewis, *Great Divorce*, IX.

5. Lewis, "A Slip," 190.

knowing good and well that God wants me to trust him, but holding the reins of trust tight to my chest in my areas of choice. Trusting God in those areas would have led to uncharted waters, and that was uncomfortable. It would have taken me deeper in my pursuit of him than my current allotment of trust would allow me to go.

When either flirting with these boundaries, or completely catapulting over them, I'd go through the exact same motions. I'd feel guilty. I'd ask forgiveness. But at the same time, I would be terrified to promise God that I would never go back to the edge. The edge was ok—no matter how many times the edge led to going overboard. The edge was my comfort zone. The edge was what I knew. Though I would never verbalize it, I trusted the edge more than I trusted God. I trusted these known pitfalls that I hated but found identity and comfort in them. This was holding me back tremendously from advancing in my walk with God. It's hard to expand one's walk with God when one is carrying around the guilt of regular sinful flirtations. I had to unclench my fist and give God what I was frightened to give. I was frightened of what my life would look like if I let go of the comforting edge. Yet, God wanted everything, *especially* those areas of my life that I was afraid to give him. I was afraid to let go of the temporal edge that Lewis flirted with as well.

I would claim to love God yet would not trust him in the areas that were uncomfortable. *Is that love?* Perhaps it was a shade of love, but not completely, and not fully.

In "On Obstinacy and Belief," Lewis discusses this, though in terms of human relationships. He discusses how loving another involves trusting them beyond the evidence, indeed even against the evidence. If one is truly going to enter a relationship with another, trust has to be freely given despite every urge to withhold it. A groom may very well not be able to produce any evidence to his new bride that he will never be unfaithful, but the trust must be given in spite of this if there ever is going to be a substantial relationship. The same is true with God. If I hand over to him the reins of my sobriety, even though I do not know what a sober tomorrow may look like (even the idea of a completely sober year terrifies me), I must trust that God will fill any void that is left in my life and fill it with something much more substantial, much more fulfilling, and much more euphoric than any liquor bottle could ever provide.

The same is true in regard to friendships. Lewis goes on to write that, "No man is our friend who believes in our good intentions only when they are proved."[6] Even in the most casual of friendships, trust is an obviously

---

6. Lewis, "On Obstinacy," 26.

vital part. I rarely invite a friend over to watch the game if I don't trust him at some level, otherwise I take the risk of him stealing from my home. The suspicious person will never be universally praised for his or her suspicion and will forever remain lonely. But the confident, trusting person displays characteristics that are universally praised, although he or she risks being hurt along the way.[7]

I knew here that Lewis was referring to the trust found in the relationship between two friends, but I knew where it was most applicable in my life. God had given me evidence that I could trust him in the past, but even where he had not, my lack of trust was unbecoming of "a friend." If my relationship with God had manifested itself as an earthly relationship, say with a girlfriend, no one would look at that relationship and describe it as anything remotely healthy. It would be viewed as suspicious, mean spirited, and self-centered. I couldn't let my relationship with God continue down this path.

I've heard it said that when we surrender our life to God, it's as if we're handing him the steering wheel of our lives. We sit passenger from now on and allow him to drive as we journey together to our destination. For most of my life I felt like I had in fact handed God the steering wheel, but my lack of trust and lack of full surrender showed its face when God took me down roads that I knew better than he. I would sit passenger only to ever-so-quickly jerk the wheel back when things got uncomfortable. Lewis helped me realize I was doing this. A key contributor to my low spiritual self-esteem was coming from my lack of surrender—my lack of trust.

I eventually got better in those areas. It's not always easy. I still reach over and grab that wheel from time to time . . . and that's ok. At least I know I'm doing it. I am still making progress. I am still moving forward, even in those moments when I seem to know the roads better than God.

My time with Lewis, my period of inner reflection, and allowing God to expand in my mind helped me let go of the temporal edge in several areas that I was not used to. The funny thing was, I would let go of the edge and trust God with a certain area of my life, and soon thereafter, a new area of sinful flirtation would illuminate: a new reoccurring thought, a new behavioral pattern or lack thereof, a better way to give of my time or resources, forgiveness that I was withholding. A new temporal edge would appear. I'd stop and I'd look up, only to see God's hand stretched out asking, "May I have that one too?" I'd have to learn to let go once more.

7. Lewis, "On Obstinacy," 26.

My former pastor Larry used to refer to this as the *Dimmer Switch Principle*.[8] The small steps of faith we take, giving God the areas of disobedience that we see right in front of us, whether passive or active disobedience, allows him to turn the dimmer switch up a little and we see more. Then we take the next step, and he turns it up a bit more. Soon our judgment grows stronger. Less of our mistake-prone humanity is able to create static on the line between ourselves and God. We enjoy God more. We see the world more as he sees it. But high-handed disobedience? That turns the dimmer switch down, and the opposite takes place. I was here for a great deal of my Christian walk. I could tell when the dimmer was down. I could tell when big issues in my walk with God were small issues, or no issue at all. The dimmer switch wasn't dim. I wasn't responding to the light I was given. My outlook grew darker. But when I began to diagnose my self-induced problem and started letting go of the edge, God turned up the dimmer switch, and I took the next step with him. I realized that this was going to be a journey, a never-ending mission to give God all that I had, even if the dimmer switch was not completely illuminated this side of eternity.

Don't get me wrong. This is not about counting sin. It's not about recording mistakes. As I explain later in this book, there's no need for us to keep a record of wrong, when God is certainly not. This has to do with realizing that our relationship with God is an active, breathing, give and take relationship. And just like any relationship, there has to be some positive movement, or it will become dark. What should be a positive—a healthy, illuminating relationship with our Creator—becomes a negative—a source of low spiritual self-esteem.

Although tomorrow will bring its challenges, and surely mistakes are bound to come, the process of learning to give my temporal clingings to God on a daily basis, no matter how large or small, is something I begin to welcome. Surely it is a mark of God's tangible working in my life. This is an example, I believe, of working out my salvation with fear and trembling, as Paul wrote about.[9]

Letting go of the lifeline of the temporal in full abandonment to Christ meant that I had to abandon any notion that full surrender to God had anything to do with my own efforts. It meant reminding myself daily that the temporal, no matter how great it might seem, simply would never fulfill. I had to trust God with what laid beyond my comfort zone. Lewis said, "Fallen man is not simply an imperfect creature who needs improvement;

8. Osborne, *Spirituality*, 71.

9. Phil 2:12.

he is a rebel who must lay down his arms."[10] Every day is a new day to wake up, try to slay the man who is desperate for the temporal, and lay down our arms once again, accepting the grace and forgiveness offered along the way.

Lewis describes God as a sea in "A Slip of the Tongue." Saint Peter describes Satan as a roaring lion, waiting for someone to devour.[11] I like these two analogies, because cats do not typically like the water. No one has ever suffered an attack from a lion while floating safely in the calm sea. One has to learn to surrender, to let go of the edge, to obey what they know, and trust God with the rest. He will show up. He will protect. The crouching lion will flee if he is resisted long enough.[12]

10. Lewis, *Mere Christianity*, 56.

11. 1 Pet 5:8.

12. Jas 4:7.

4

Afraid of Surrender

Hand over the whole natural self, all the desires which you think innocent as well as the ones you think wicked . . . I will give you a new self instead. In fact, I will give you Myself.

—C. S. Lewis, *Mere Christianity*[1]

M Y lack of trust was ultimately stemming from a lack of complete and full surrender. I was a follower of Christ, who loved and generally wanted to follow him, but my lack of complete surrender would routinely cause me to "go home to bury my father first."[2]

To C. S. Lewis, Christianity eventually made so much sense that anything less than complete surrender to God was intellectually dishonest. In his famous Liar, Lunatic, or Lord trilemma, the mere fact that Jesus was not a Liar or a Lunatic left inquirers only one option: to fall at his feet and call him Lord and God.[3] Logically, it made more sense that Lewis fall at the feet of Christ and surrender his whole self rather than not. It was not an emotional choice; it was the logical next step. The rational thing to do was to surrender to God. Yet, anyone who makes this choice, whether it be logical or emotional, is in for some major reconstruction if they allow it. Christ will radically alter any area of one's life that is offered to him. The goal is to offer to him everything.

1. Lewis, *Mere Christianity*, 196.
2. Luke 9:59.
3. Lewis, *Mere Christianity*, 52.

"Surrender" is a theme of C. S. Lewis. He has many themes, but the importance of complete surrender to the truth found in Christianity, once realized, makes an appearance in just about every book, devotion, or essay he ever penned. In "A Slip of the Tongue" Lewis writes:

> It is not so much of our time and so much of our attention that God demands; it is not even all our time and all our attention: it is ourselves. [4]

Surrender is not giving God all of our time and attention. It's not giving him more time in the pews, more devotions in the morning, less premarital sex at night. It's giving him ourselves, our whole selves—the dirt, the grime, the debauchery—and trusting that he loves us regardless.

In "A Slip of the Tongue" Lewis goes on to say that God will be forever merciful to our chronic failures and our repeated mistakes, but he never accepts deliberate compromise. We must never plant our flag in the enemy's territory. We must never accept our humanity. We must be found in resistance.[5] The mistakes in our lives may accompany us to our deathbeds but let us all say that we fought the good fight in the battle against them.

I enjoy this section from "A Slip of the Tongue" because Lewis deals with two things people like myself drastically need to know. For one, I am one of those Christians whose repeated failures are a constant source of low spiritual self-esteem. It is not the brand new mistakes that creep into my life that put me in my condition, although they may take me by surprise, it is the repeated failures that have convinced me of my low standing on the perpetual spiritual totem pole; those failures I've asked forgiveness for last week, last month, and last year, yet still seem to make a routine appearance in my life. But here Lewis reminds me that the best position I can put myself in is to simply be in the resistance, not to have to achieve some unattainable, mistake-free lifestyle.

"He will be infinitely merciful to our repeated failures"—but I must be in the resistance.[6] This was great news. Being in the resistance is much more attainable than being entirely without. All my life I saw the process of removing sin entirely as a mark of spiritual maturity. As a fundamentalist, this seemed to be the implied goal: not enjoying my walk with God, but constantly battling to remove all remaining iniquities. Christianity was a fearful, cleaning process, not an enchanting trusting process. This mindset will always leave us sinful creatures coming up short. We will always see

---

4. Lewis, "A Slip," 189.
5. Lewis, "A Slip," 189.
6. Lewis, "A Slip," 189.

the ground that is yet to cover and not the ground that has been covered by Christ. But here Lewis reminds us that simply being in the resistance could equally be a mark of spiritual maturity. There seems to be a chink in the armor of low spiritual self-esteem.

I read "A Slip of the Tongue" and stopped asking myself whether I was winning or losing—had I instead given up? Was I still in the resistance? The mere fact that I was fighting through these questions proved that I was assuredly in the resistance. No matter how far away from God I felt, there was still a breath of air in my spiritual life. I had not held up my spiritual surrender flag. I was still in the fight and that meant I was much further along in my walk with Christ than my emotions allowed me to believe. This was a new area of thought for me. All my life I have thought entirely in black and white. Lewis began to allow a little gray into my world view, and it felt good.

Lewis also reminds Christians like me that surrendering to God eventually means there will be nothing of our own left to live on. Surrendering to God means I am surrendering the ordinary life that I cling to, love, and keep a death-grip on. Knowing that complete surrender to God eventually means giving up on the expectations of an ordinary life helps me begin to be free from the fear of not having what others may consider a normal life.

For example, by this point in my life I expected to be married. I have longed to be married and have tried very hard to be so. This passion has occasionally taken precedence over what I know God would have me do. A sizable portion of the mistakes and emotional baggage that I have picked up in my adult life stem from trying to make a relationship work with the wrong girl or, more often than not, a great girl that I dated prematurely, before I was in a healthy enough place to be involved romantically. I have played the same scenario out countless times in my life. I find a seemingly wonderful woman, yet, because of my tiresome ability to be focused on the temporal, coupled with my desire to be married, I try to jam a square peg into a round hole, and end up with the same results every time: brokenness, damaged feelings, and eventually, singleness, again. Because being married (especially in professional ministry) is considered ordinary, I was forcing my will over God's in order to achieve it. However, knowing that full surrender to God might possibly mean giving up the ordinary lets out the steam of forcing something that God, in his sovereignty, may not be ready to give to me.

In an essay called "The Christian View on Suffering," Lewis writes,

"Imagine a set of people all living in the same building. Half of them think it is a hotel, the other half think it is a prison. Those who think it a hotel might regard it as quite intolerable, and those who thought it was a prison might decide that it was really surprisingly comfortable."[7]

It really is all about managing one's expectations. Being in the line of work I am in introduces me to a lot of prisoners. I have allowed some former inmates the opportunity to spend a few days in my house upon their release. I have seen firsthand their reaction to sleeping in my guest room which is, by all practical purposes, the most boring and unaccommodating room in my house. It also holds the smallest, most uncomfortable twin bed the mattress companies ever connived—my cat barely finds it suitable. Yet, the ex-inmates have always slept like babies. I've heard comments like, "That's the first time I've slept all through the night in several years." They wake up to coffee with smiles on their faces. My expectations and their expectations are quite different. Their mindset is one of contentment and gratitude. Mine is one of, "Let me give this bed to the cat, because neither me or my son is touching it."

Maybe surrendering to God includes managing my expectations: doing what I know to be right, being in the resistance of what I know to be wrong, trusting him with the results, and holding on to no expectations of the ordinary. Jesus says, "If the world hates you, keep in mind that I hated me first."[8] If I expect a prison cell in this life, that is ok, but I should be quite happy if it turns out to be a hotel.

The Kilns

I walked past Lewis's home in Oxford, which displayed the name "The Kilns," towards the walking trail that Lewis would stroll down often to start his day, clear his head, or walk off his writer's block. It was beautiful. No wonder Lewis was so happy to have landed this property. The greenery in this lush forest looked like something straight out of Hobbiton. Appropriately enough, Lewis and Tolkien spent many a day walking down these trails, talking about literature and mythology and swimming together in the pond. I could only imagine the stories that this tranquil place inspired; stories that we have the pleasure of reading today, and many that we do not. The majestic trees arched above my head, creating a canopy shadow on the

---

7. Lewis, "Christian View," 103–4.

8. John 15:8.

dirt path in front of my boots. I started thinking about how beautiful this piece of property was and how happy I was that it remained intact. And then, as per normal, when a human heart is confronted with such a piece of quiet serenity, my heart moved to something higher. My heart moved to God.

I didn't say anything. I did not even formulate words in my mind that I wanted to fire in his direction. I just let my heart enjoy him. Lewis writes, "Prayer without words is the best."[9] I certainly agreed with him that day. I had come too far in my spiritual journey to muck up this moment with any words, requests, or repentance. I just enjoyed my Creator. God knows the posture of our heart, much more than we give him credit for. The psalmists certainly understood this. Sometimes I think we just need quiet solitude to open up our raw hearts to him and let him explore them. Just be still. Just listen. Stop talking. There are no awkward silences between us and God. Let him search the depths of our souls and pull out exactly what our hearts are thirsty to lay before him. Or at least, that's a way I connect with him. I know we're all different.

I eventually made my way around the crystal pond and back down the trail that led to the Kilns. I paused for a second outside the front door of the house to look at the elevated flower garden behind me. I recalled a black and white picture of Lewis and his wife, Joy, sitting out here in their chairs, Lewis enjoying his cigarette, Joy enjoying her knitting . . . both enjoying each other. I smiled briefly, turned around, and walked into Lewis's home.

The C. S. Lewis Foundation had taken great pains to make sure they kept the original look and feel of the house. Restoration projects had concluded in 2001. It felt like a warm place to call home. Lewis found contentment here. It even smelled like bacon and eggs upon entering the initial hallway. (Come to find out the Foundation allows Oxford students to stay there during their studies, as long as they keep the house up to standards, only live in certain rooms of the house, and do not mind the occasional tourist popping in. So, the bacon and eggs were real bacon and eggs coming from a student named Tommy, cooking on Lewis's stove. I'm sure Lewis would not have minded.)

The library to my left was vast. There was a Narnia map framed on the wall above the fire place. I doubt that this map was there in Lewis's day, but I suppose tourists like myself expected to see something of Narnia when arriving at C. S. Lewis's home. A desk was scooted up against the window. I could imagine Lewis sitting there, writing a lecture or an essay, watching his wife work the garden. I knew in all actuality they had a professional

9. Lewis, *Letters to Malcom,* 11.

gardener come to their home to manhandle all the shrubbery, but it was a nice thought.

I made my way down the hall, where I met up with some of my classmates and a student in the house in charge of giving tours. While I do not recall her name, I do remember that she was a very nice girl—a petite, redheaded girl of around twenty. Her knowledge of Lewis and his home life was extensive, and while she was actually an American student from Maine, a curious English accent had begun to take root. She pointed out that the ceilings had been painted a yellowish, drab color to keep the integrity of the condition it was in. Lewis, his brother, and all his Oxford mates sat in this library—joking, laughing, smoking pipes and cigarettes that regularly sent a barrage of tobacco smoke up, leaving a discolored ceiling that probably started off as white. Thank goodness they did not leave the ashes on floor, which Lewis was known for dumping on the ground, never seeing the need for an ashtray. He was a bachelor for quite some time.

The idea of surrender was on my mind that day. I'd been thinking about the concept of complete surrender to God and what that looks like most of my time at Oxford and Cambridge. I was intellectually honest with myself. I knew at many times in my life I was not living in complete surrender as I covered above, and I knew that was a cause of my low spiritual self-esteem which, at that time in England, I had come so far towards overcoming . . . and here I was. I was in the home of a man whose life was fully and completely surrendered to God once he became intellectually honest with himself.

Lewis loved this home and property and felt deeply appreciative to own it. He never dreamed he would be able own such a piece of land. Yet, although Lewis felt blessed to have such a beautiful home, in the back of his active mind, he was always a little worried about his finances. He never did amass a large amount of savings. Why? It's not because he did not make enough. He certainly had a decent amount coming in during a time that Great Britain had a war-induced, shaky economy. No, he was unable to build great wealth because he gave. He gave, and he gave some more—his money, his time, and his home.

He and the Kilns became the caretaker to many who needed his support, including his brother who struggled with alcoholism and his late best friend's mother, Mrs. Moore, whom Lewis had supported since coming home from World War I. He continued to support her well into her dementia, even as her attitude began to wear on his emotions and well-being. He took in children from London whose lives were affected by the London bombings of World War II. He would come home on his lunch breaks to walk whichever dogs Mrs. Moore happened to bring home at the time. He returned every piece of fan mail he possibly could, so much so that whole volumes of literature today are comprised of Lewis's correspondence with fans from all over the world and of all different ages. Despite the stunted growth his Christian-themed books brought to his professional career at Oxford, Lewis still took the time to translate the hard-to-grasp theological, apologetical, and philosophical concepts into something the common man could understand. He gave everything of value that he had to give . . . including the home that I was walking through.

Lewis understood the dangers of material possessions. That's why he was able to hold his treasures in an open palm. He writes in *The Screwtape Letters*, "Prosperity knits a man to the world. He feels that he is finding his place in it, while really it is finding its place in him."[10] This entanglement was one that Lewis intended to avoid. As Lewis's star began to rise as a writer and public speaker, he began to receive royalties from his first few published books and his radio broadcasts on the BBC. This money he gave away in its entirety. He donated all the royalties to a clergy widows fund. Eventually, as more books were published, aided by his good friend Owen Barfield, Lewis set up a trust called the Agape Fund, in which two thirds of all of Lewis's royalties were distributed to charities, widows, Oxford students in need, churches, and many other ministries—and to top it off, Lewis's name was far detached from these generous gifts. Lewis had no intentions on ever boasting in his giving. In *Mere Christianity*, he made the point that the temptation to be showy in our charity is also a temptation that needs to be recognized and fought against. Things like tipping and hospitality, while great in and of themselves, can damper the need to give to those who really need our help.[11] Lewis kept his charitable giving between himself and God. It's safe to say that if he had a social media account, we would not be scrolling through all the photos of him helping the needy. We would have never known.

Only a man fully surrendered to God can give away two thirds of his royalties while still having those familiar worries of financial ruin in the back of his mind, like many of us carry today. This is a picture of what surrender looks like, I believe: not complete security, but complete trust. Lewis writes in a letter to his routine correspondence friend, Mary, that he is not worried that on his deathbed he'll reflect that he was a sucker for giving his money away to anyone that asks. He would not regret if he responded to a hoax with charity, but it would haunt him to think that he refused even one person in need. He goes on to write, "*Another thing that annoys me is when people say 'Why did you give that man money? He'll probably go and drink*

---

10. Lewis, *Screwtape Letters*, 155.
11. Lewis, *Mere Christianity*, 86–87.

it.' My reply is 'But if I'd kept it I should probably have drunk it.'[12] This is an example of a man, with all the worries, skepticisms, and temptations of the flesh, in complete surrender to God. This was one area of the temporal edge that Lewis was able to release, so he could float off into the sea that is God.

I walked into a large gathering room built onto the back of the house where the Foundation had kept and preserved the original sign for the Eagle and Child pub. I took a picture of the marriage license on the wall that legally bound Clive Staples Lewis and Joy Davidman and sat there and enjoyed some great conversation about what that home was like during its heyday, throughout the hustle and bustle of visitors, relatives, random dogs, and refugees.

Eventually I traveled through Lewis's brother Warnie's room, where liquor bottles of all sorts were strung about to retell the story of the addiction that he suffered with a large portion of his adult life, despite his full adherence to Christianity.

I walked past a hand-carved, detailed mahogany wardrobe, stepped up a narrow staircase into an office, and sat down at the desk where he had penned all seven books of The Chronicles of Narnia. I took a moment to let it set in as much as it could—the joy that this desk had brought countless children of all ages. (I considered penning an eighth book but realized we were short on time.)

I got up and followed a plaque on the wall that read, "C. S. Lewis's Bedroom." I leaned on the side of the open doorway. It was a small, unassuming room that most people today would consider a decent sized storage closet. I looked at the staircase outside of the window that Lewis used to get in and out of his house during the blistering cold as he had lost a very important key to the front door. This remained his routine until he got married and Joy had the epiphany to hire a locksmith. Joy was good for Lewis.

It is hard to walk through that house without having a bit of joy in one's heart. It was hard for me to walk through without reminding myself that trust, and complete surrender to God, means floating off into the unknown but loving him enough to know that he will be there waiting to meet me on the distant shore. The water around me will become sweeter and more crystal clear than I have ever seen. I'll float further up and further in. Closer and closer to Aslan's Country.

~

12. Lewis, *Yours, Jack*, 60–61.

During Lewis's famous broadcast speeches on the BBC Radio during World War II, which were eventually compiled and edited to makeup his signature work, *Mere Christianity*, he spoke about this idea of surrender and what God will do for us if we allow him.

He uses the example of a us as a living house that has recently given God permission to do some slight renovations on. We expect him to chip around the edges. We expect him to replace our drains, to stop the leaks, and so on. We know those areas of us need attention when we first hand God the keys, and we fully expect him to dilly-dally in those areas. But then he decides to take out a wall that we aren't expecting. Then he takes a sledge hammer to some tile that we are just fine with. We're confused, and perhaps questioning God's ability to properly renovate a home. What is God up to? Does he know what he's doing? Did I know what I was doing when I allowed him to renovate me?

The answer, of course, is that God is building something out of us that we were not expecting. He is taking down walls in our lives that we were not prepared for him to knock down. He has a very different blueprint in mind than the rest of us do. All of a sudden God starts adding on wings, new floors, and courtyards. [13] Lewis concludes:

> You thought you were being made into a decent little cottage: but He is building a palace. He intends to come and live in it Himself. [14]

Opening the door to God, even a little, allows him to come in and make sweeping changes. In my case, Christ had radically altered every area of my life that I have given him. Yet, as previously mentioned, there were several areas of my life that I refused to give him. These were the known temptations in my life: the glaring flaws not so glaring; the areas of my life I stored in the back of my mind because truly dealing with them would require some major reconstruction, and I would rather not for the time being; the weapons I refused to lay down, denying God the housecleaning he wanted to do and the peace of mind he wanted to bring. These roads were familiar. God had pointed them out to me several times. I had been at the end of them several times, only to plea for forgiveness every time. But what would have happened if I just strolled by that road instead of going down it? Obviously, the road was tempting, or else I would not find myself on it so often.

13. Lewis, *Mere Christianity*, 86–87.
14. Lewis, *Mere Christianity*, 86–87.

Lewis writes, "A man who gives into temptation after five minutes simply does not know what it would have been like an hour later."[15] When it came to my reoccurring mistakes, what would have happened if I would have kept moving forward for five more minutes instead of turning down a road previously known by me to end in disaster? Well, thanks to Lewis and some great mentors in my life, I eventually pushed past some of those off-ramps.

One temptation that Lewis's writings helped me overcome was that of keeping all of my money for myself. I'm not here to discuss what the Bible says about tithing, but one cannot read Scripture and walk away with any other notion than God wants us to give something to the poor, or an organization that will do so in our stead—10 percent, 20 percent, 100 percent—it does not matter. What matters is the posture of our heart whenever we are giving to others. Lewis had this area of surrender down. I however did not.

Giving my money has been traditionally harder for me than giving my time. (Although I do believe there are people that God would rather give their time than money, but for me that's never been a problem.) It's not that I'm a miser. No, I'm much worse. I'm an extreme budgeter. Every last dime from my paycheck has a place to go. With every paycheck I designate a certain amount towards groceries, a certain amount towards entertainment, a certain amount towards gas, and so on. The amount I was going to give to my church or a charity was already baked into the numbers. Every month I would pull up my color-coded spreadsheet, preloaded with all the formulas that would calculate all expenditures down to the last cent, and I would command all my money where to go. It is a beautiful sight to see actually. One number goes down, the other goes up. However, for the longest time, every time I was budgeting I would get this nagging sensation that God wanted me to give more than I already was, but the temptation to keep my money in its predetermined assignments was stronger than the voice of God for a period of my life. It was an actual temptation that came, not from being a Scrooge with my finances, but more from not wanting to interrupt my system of money in, money out that I had got down to a science. Giving extra to someone or something else simply did not fit with any of my overall goals. Yet, the nagging feeling remained. The monthly temptation to keep more of my money and ignore that faint voice was one that I obeyed like clockwork.

But one day I started thinking, *what if I just did it?* Lewis's words moved from the back of my head to the front. I thought, *what if I just fought through this temptation of keeping all of my paycheck without thinking about it?* Like Lewis reminded, I would have no idea what that temptation would be like

15. Lewis, *Mere Christianity*, 142.

an hour later. A week later. A year later. *What if I just punched through this temptation without thinking about it?* Remember, I had chosen to quasi-relaunch my relationship with God, and that meant following the soft voice I knew to be his. I had made a commitment to turn the dimmer switch up, and Lewis was coaching me. *I would have no idea what the temptation would be like an hour later. What if I just walked by the road of temptation instead of taking the recognizable path straight down it?*

My mentor Eric reminded me one day that Muhammad Ali doesn't even start counting his sit-ups until they start hurting. When the pain kicks in, that's when he starts counting. It's through our pain that we bring about real-life change. I had been flirting with this idea of giving for far too long, and it had landed me nowhere. If I truly wanted to start anew with God, and allow Lewis to help me, it was time to let myself suffer some pain. So, I did it. It was painful, but I did it.

I pulled up a charitable organization's website, one that I had been a fan of for quite some time and made a donation that in no way fit into my spreadsheet. With one swift click on my laptop I had disrupted the color-coded symphony that was my budgeting spreadsheet. Lewis was practically leaning over my shoulder, reminding me, "A man who gives into temptation after five minutes simply does not know what it would have been like an hour later." Well, an hour later, I was feeling just fine. A week later, I was feeling just fine.

The temptation to hoard all of my money for myself has dispersed over time. I listened to the light that I had. Lewis laid something on my heart, and God reminded me about it until I budged. The dimmer switch went up. My giving has increased and works well within the spreadsheet system. While I still have some room to grow in my ability to give, my ability to punch through temptation has grown tremendously—one more area of my life that I knew good and well was not surrendered.

Giving is obviously just an example. It was brought to my attention simply because it was an area of my life that I was holding back from God. I'm sure those areas are different for everyone. The areas of our life that we need to surrender to him will ebb and flow with our different stages of life. The goal is to listen to that still, small voice. When we do, it will increasingly grow louder.

For the first time ever, I actually started handing over the areas of my life that I knew Christ wanted the most and began to trust him with the re-sults. While I was still far away, the good news is that I knew it. The excuses were beginning to fade. I had dirt all over my face because of my lack of full surrender, but now I could see it. Finally looking in the mirror is a great first step to washing the dirt off one's face.

5

Blinded by Moralism

We know nothing of religion here: we think only of Christ . . .
—C. S. LEWIS, *THE GREAT DIVORCE*[1]

W E Western Christians can be a very determined people. We often take pride in a "can-do" attitude, a "be all that you can be" mindset. When we've grown sick and tired of being sick and tired, it's easy for us to draw a line in the sand and become determined to fix ourselves, determined to become better parents, better leaders, determined to pull ourselves up by the bootstraps and fix any issues that are plaguing us. This is by no means a bad thing. It has led many out of poverty, many into better health, etc., but when that self-determination bleeds into our Christian culture, that "can-do" attitude, at times, can be a spiritually fatal mindset, blinding us of what we are desperately in need of.

In Lewis's *The Great Divorce*, a busload of tourists from hell travel to heaven with the possibility of staying if they would simply surrender to God—even a "germ of a desire" for God would suffice. While there are many surprises found in this important book, and many examples of people we would recognize in today's culture, one of the most surprising aspects of this story are the religious people both on this bus and in the gray town below (hell). Religious people are living in hell; religious people are still organizing, still having theology meetings, still trying to do a good job building a church. Religious people are still waiting for their version of Jesus to show up, save the day, justify their way of life, and set them free, under their terms.

1. Lewis, *Great Divorce*, 42.

They are blinded. They are, as Lewis describes in this book, "so occupied in spreading Christianity they never gave a thought to Christ."[2] They are great leaders and teachers with great morals that would put the best of us to shame. They are committed to their religion but not committed to Christ.

Chances are these religious folks built a great church in the gray town below—a church that had a deep theology society, active Sunday school classes, the best dressed people, and multiple services to fit everyone. Chances are they had engaging, emotional worship, equipped with all the best prerecorded hooks, lights, and smoke. Chances are they had great lessons that sprinkled in a Bible verse or two, and maybe all their application points all started with the same letter. Yet, Christ's ransom for their battered souls was not being preached—moral behavior was. (For the record, I am not against emotional theology societies, Sunday school, multiple worship services with smoke and lights, nor am I anti messages with uniformed application points. I quite enjoy them and experience God through them.) The reason I bring this up is because the focus on morality, and not Christ's redeeming blood on the cross, was a large source of my low spiritual self-esteem. It can be a dangerous trap for those who love God and sincerely want to follow Christ yet place a great deal of weight on their moral performance.

Placing too much emphasis on what we did wrong, instead of what God has done right can be a recipe for spiritual failure. Placing too much emphasis on what we do right, instead of what Christ accomplished on the cross, is also a recipe for spiritual failure. If we forget that heaven is being filled with tax collectors and prostitutes,[3] we're prone to overlook our own brokenness and believe than somehow, because we've achieved some kind of high moral ground, we are better that those people. We definitely are not. We are just as in desperate need of the cross as they are. In fact, sometimes they may be nearer to the cross—as Lewis reminds us, "Those that hate goodness are sometimes nearer than those that know nothing at all about it and think that they have it already."[4]

If moral behavior is being taught in our Christian culture without the grace of God whenever we fail to live up to that moral behavior, it is a precursor for self-loathing people to become even more self-loathing. I was here for years and years. I was surrounded by this in the pulpits, in bookstores, and by speakers at conferences who were extremely gifted when it came time to speak on topics such as willpower, discipline, and morality. This undoubtedly aided my less-than feelings about how well I was doing at

2. Lewis, *Great Divorce*, 74.

3. Matt 21–31.

4. Lewis, *Great Divorce*, 82.

being a Christian. All I could see was the behavior I struggled to live up to and not the grace that blanketed me regardless.

In Lewis's *The Screwtape Letters*, Screwtape (a high-ranking demon in hell's chain of command) has a plan to distract men's mind from what Christ did on the cross and turn Jesus into a great moral teacher. He knew that we all have a primeval moral code in our hearts that a good teacher can tap into and rally church members around. He knew that if church members were rallying around moral behavior more than surrendering their flawed souls to Christ, then one point is scored by "Our Father Below."[5] Why would a demon want to make church members more moral? I suppose because it still leaves us in the driver seat. Moral behavior for the sake of moral behavior will never hand over the wheel to God. It takes our dependence off of Christ and leaves us in control. That's much more of a comfortable spot for us morally-determined people than dependence on another is.

Lewis writes in "A Slip of the Tongue":

> Will it really make no difference whether it was women or patriotism, cocaine or art, whisky or a seat in the Cabinet, money or science? Well, surely no difference that matters. We shall have missed the end for which we are formed and rejected the only thing that satisfies. Does it matter to a man dying in a desert by which choice of route he missed the only well?[6]

People don't tend take their car into the shop unless they see, feel, or hear an issue with it. When we're convinced that we're leading a pretty moral life, the need for repair is diminished. If Screwtape can get us addicted to our own moral dependence, our dependence on God will never be realized. We could easily live for something else. I wonder how many people will realize they live for morality, a church, or for cultural Christianity when they could have easily been living for sex, patriotism, cocaine, or art.

The moral behavior du jour can be very enticing and scratch us right where we itch, especially if the speaker is particularly skillful and motivating. While much of the message might ring true, if we're not careful, all we will get is motivation that puts the onus of moralism on us, without the constant reminder that we are in fact very imperfect people; imperfect people who will probably let ourselves down or let others down sometime

---

5. Screwtape's title for the devil in Lewis, *Screwtape Letters*.

6. Lewis, "A Slip," 191.

in the very near future. Only the cross of Christ can mend that gap, and we need to be reminded of that on a daily basis.

Our fascination with moralism can easily put us at a disadvantage. The need for Christ can easily be diminished when our Christian faith gets masqueraded behind our current moral standard. It is very easy to surrender to a culture of moralism without ever having surrendered to Christ. If moral behavior becomes our goal, and not Christ, in whom we can only meet in our brokenness, it can be dangerously blinding. I'd rather be an addict who can see that I need Jesus than a religious man who is blind.

I want to be careful here because I am very much in favor of constant improvement. There is nothing wrong with wanting to shore up our behavior and morality. There is nothing wrong with churches teaching moral habits and traits, based on Scripture. Who else should be doing that if not our churches? There is also nothing wrong with wanting to be a better leader and a cleaner, more productive member of society. In fact, Scripture is clear that we are to work on ourselves in an attempt to become more Christ-like. But it is also clear Christ mends the gap wherever we fail. It's clear that prostitutes and tax collectors are entering into heaven before morally religious people.[7] It's even clear that a lifelong criminal can profess his faith in Christ and enter into paradise,[8] having never stepped foot in a church or displayed the slightest bit of moral behavior. We need to make sure we are attaching God's provisions to the appeal to change our behavior. Some people are better at change than others. Some people will struggle with change their entire lives . . . and Christ's blood covers them all. We need to be reminded daily.

Indeed, broken people depending on Christ for their salvation is a much more desirable position than moral people depending on their own behavior. Christ has nailed our sinful natures to a cross. That should be just as encouraging as a "you have what it takes" book.

After years of being constantly reminded of my humanity by my inability to not screw things up, I had to learn to relax. I had to learn to truly trust the power of God to forgive all my shortcomings, past, present, and future—the ones that I knew about and the ones I did not know about. I also had to learn that there's no use in hiding my humanity. Why would it ever be sociably acceptable to hide our humanity from other flawed humans? Why not be a bunch of sinners, saved by grace? Whenever we can all relax and

7. Matt 21:31.
8. Luke 23:39–43.

accept that premise, that's when the masks come off. That's when healing begins. That's when real relationships begin—more on that later.

I had to learn to be cautious of the man in the mirror, when I would truly *believe in me* and profess that *I have what it takes*. Sometimes I do—a lot of times I do not. I have routinely proved to myself that I do not. If I am in the business of cleaning up my moral performance while forgetting about and relying upon the power of the cross to cover all of my mistakes regardless of that performance, I am in danger of surrendering to my Christian culture while not surrendering to Christ. I am in danger of surrendering to moral behavior but not to Christ. The thief on the cross did not have the opportunity to change one thing about his performance before he entered paradise. My trust must be in Christ, not in myself. Closer union with him must be my goal, not a moral life. The moralism will take care of itself as I fall more in love with him for mending the gap between me and perfection. I will learn to love and trust him more, and thus, "obey his commands,"[9] resulting in that moral life being touted on stages across the world.

I don't mean to be too hard on our Christian culture. All of our churches, organizations, ministries, authors, and speakers are all human. We are all equally messed up people, and when messed up people run any organization, even a church, it is going to be flawed. If love truly does look over a multitude of sins, I have no grounds for judging any church, culture, or the people in it. I love and deeply respect my church and its staff. I also love and deeply respect the churches and staffs that I have been involved with in the past. They are doing more for the kingdom than I could ever hope. However, in my own personal walk with Christ, I've made it a promise to never get so caught up in my ability to fix my own moral behavior that I forget about Christ and his redemptive work. I would never want anyone to say of me that I was so occupied in spreading Christianity (or morality, or a church, or a brand) that I never gave a thought to Christ. I've made it my personal mission to improve myself in many different facets, including morality, but to never put the blinders on; to always remain broken and in need of a savior; to never allow the lines to be blurred between great moral repair and the only one who can truly fix me. He's much better at repair than I.

Eventually, the more I began to get in touch with the darkness inside, the more I came to terms with the fact that sin was constantly lurking directly beneath everyone's skin no matter how well we dressed that day. I had to learn to be cautious of my attempts at moralism. I had to learn to be cautious of my "can-do" attitude and be able to recognize it when it crept up. When it comes to moral behavior, maybe I "can-do." Maybe I cannot.

9. John 14:15.

Regardless, Jesus did. And in this I place my hope. Shooting for high morals is great. If it blinds us to our deeply rooted, desperate need for daily grace and restoration, it can be detrimental to our souls.

An unfortunate byproduct of being blinded by moralism is the unholy guilt that accompanies it. When the inevitable mistake does occur, it carries more weight than it should. When I am up to my neck in moralism, and not the grace and restoration of Christ, my failures are highlighted, and an unhealthy amount of guilt is the result. The opposite of pride is always guilt and either one can creep into the Christian's life when he or she is more focused on moral behavior than they are the redeeming work of the cross. I've learned that feeling guilty is equally as toxic to one's spiritual health as pride.

Guilt has very little place in a Christian's life. It is necessary only in that it brings us to God and to others in repentance. After that it becomes toxic and, dare I say, sinful. In July 1958, in a letter to a friend he corresponded with in America, Lewis writes:

> Remember what St. John says: 'If our heart condemns us, God is stronger than our heart.' The feeling of being, or not being, forgiven and loved, is not what matters.[10]

Feelings have absolutely nothing to do with whether or not God has forgiven us. Just like Lewis says above, God is stronger than our hearts that condemn us. He is stronger than our emotions, our unstable minds, our bad diets, our messed-up childhoods, our strive for perfection, our fear of failure, our disapproving relatives, and our disapproving selves. God is stronger than it all.

Lewis goes on to write to his American friend about what he called "brass tacks." If a certain sin is disrupting our relationship with God and others, confess it and move on. Otherwise "tell the despondent devil not to be silly."[11] We cannot help but hear his annoying voice, constantly motivated to condemn us. It is much like the extreme tinnitus I have. There is a constant ringing in both of my ears. The good news is I have grown accustomed to it. It is only annoying when I pay it a bit of attention. Otherwise, it disappears behind all the sounds I choose to focus on. Lewis described the silly devil's voice the same way, like an "odious inner radio." He encouraged his

10. Lewis, *Yours, Jack*, 312.
11. Lewis, *Yours, Jack*, 312.

pen-pal to treat it merely as that—as an annoying buzzing in her ear, or any other nuisance. [12]

The ringing in our ears may continue. The buzzing of the odious inner radio may pursue. Our heart may continue to condemn. The man in the mirror may continue in his dirty looks. Our feelings may ebb and flow, but God is bigger than all of that. Who am I to assign the cross a lower place on the spiritual totem pole that is my ever-changing emotions?

Here, Lewis taught me to check my guilt at the door. He also demanded that I treat any nagging guilt, that continuous reminder that I am a third-string Christian, like the tinnitus that I daily choose to ignore. Christ has already taken my inevitable sinful failures and done away with them. Again, the healing balm that was Lewis's enormous view of God continues to take effect in my life.

The religious people on the bus and in the gray town below were blinded. They were blinded by their own efforts and attempts to reach God by following all the rules. When one can actually check off all three of the application points of the pastor's last message, the need for a savior starts to diminish, and unassuming pride will begin to fill the gap where that need once was. Like the Pharisees of Old who would take great pride in being able to check off all 613 laws that elevated them above everyone else. Yet, the need for a savior remained unrecognized. Moral people do not need a savior—broken people do. *God help us to stay broken.*

Dabbling in the shallow end of God, being afraid to let go in full surrender, and being blinded by the moralism that can so easily replace a relationship with God can all be severe causes of low spiritual self-esteem—these, of course, are aided by an elementary view of God and a low view of self. At this point, it's time to talk about the fun stuff: *The Remedies.* I picked a few of my favorite remedies down below, but this is by no means an exhaustive list. They are simply a drop in the bucket of the onslaught of remedies that Lewis provided to help cure this low view of my spiritual self.

---

12. Lewis, *Yours, Jack*, 312.

PART 3

Essays on the Remedies

6

Removing the Dragon Skin

"Then the lion said—but I don't know if it spoke—'You will have to let me undress you.' I was afraid of his claws, I can tell you, but I was pretty nearly desperate now. So I just lay flat down on my back to let him do it."

—EUSTACE SCRUBB, *THE VOYAGE OF THE DAWN TREADER*[1]

READ *The Voyage of the Dawn Treader.* In this classic installment of *The Chronicles of Narnia*, Lewis tells the story of Eustace Clarence Scrubb, a character who would make appearances in three of the Narnia books. In short, Eustace was a very disagreeable boy in *The Dawn Treader.* He was a spoiled, somewhat nasty little boy who weighed heavy on everyone around him. For the first half of his journey through Narnia, he was clearly focused inwardly, showing disregard to anyone who was not name Eustace Clarence Scrubb. His selfishness was so much that it eventually led him to a very undesirable condition.

The crew of the Dawn Treader had made a brief landing at an island in order to wash themselves, find food, and make some much-needed repairs to the ship. Eustace, while trying to avoid the mundane nuisance of ship repair work, slipped away to enjoy some alone time. On his journey to find a descent to rest he stumbled upon a substantial supply of a dragon's treasure, a dragon that he would come to find out had died. In front of Eustace was an overabundance of gold, silver, jewelry, and crowns. As might be expected, the greed and lust for the exquisite collection overcame the lad and he gave

1. Lewis, *Voyage of* Dawn, 104.

in. Not only did he fill his arms and his pockets with the precious loot, he also filled his heart. It overcame him, so much so that he fell asleep on top of it. As he slipped into a longer and deeper slumber, his outward appearance slowly began to change into a form that better matched his inward appearance. Upon waking up, Eustace realized, to his horror, that he had become a dragon himself.

For brevity's sake, I will just say that Eustace went through a range of emotions with his newfound situation. At first, he was quite pleased and quite eager to display the dominance that comes with being a ferocious dragon. Eventually, however, he wanted the dragon skin removed. He missed his friends—albeit this was the first time he had ever considered them as such. He missed being useful aboard the Dawn Treader, even though he probably never actually was. For likely the first point in his life, Eustace was desiring to be a team player. He desired friendship and the opportunity to look beyond himself. He wanted to change. After a lifetime of giving into the temptations of greed and inward focus, he had become something hideous, with little traces of himself left. He wanted it removed. He did not like who he had become. He wanted to be better, inwardly and outwardly. We will leave Eustace here for now and return later.

Every day we are taking small steps towards an eventual outcome. We are taking small steps in either the right direction or the wrong direction. We are either becoming something quite lovely or something quite horrid. We are slowly becoming something quite angelic or something quite demonic. This journey of a few small steps, either gradually becoming something hideous and beastly after a lifetime of living for oneself, or gradually becoming something grand and beautiful after a lifetime of living for God and others, is a topic Lewis likes to address. It makes an appearance in several of Lewis's works, both devotional and nonfiction. Lewis thinks that every day people are taking small steps towards an eventual reality. Even the most uninteresting, dull person we encounter will one day "be a creature which, if you saw it now, you would be strongly tempted to worship, or else a horror and a corruption such as you now meet, if at all, only in a nightmare."[2] Lewis was very in tune with the eventual reality of our everyday small decisions. He writes, "All day long we are, in some degree, helping each other to one or other of these destinations."[3]

2. Lewis, "Weight of Glory," 45–46.
3. Lewis, "Weight of Glory," 45–46.

We do not start off horrid. We do not start off angelic. We may feel the soft whisper to give a bit of our time or money to the poor, just as an example, but a simple rejection of that whisper leads to one small step towards the horrid. Eventually the whisper disappears. We cannot hear the slightest bit of urging. We become more inwardly focused. We become hard. We start to blame others for our condition and are extremely angry at those who are not inwardly focused. Yet when we listen to the whisper, we take a small step towards the angelic. The whisper becomes louder. There's an inner joy. When people see us, they know we are living a life bigger than ourselves. They may praise us for it or hate us for it, but they know there is something positive within us. After giving in towards the whisper time and time again, it eventually amplifies to a beautiful scream, and we live a life that is very outwardly focused—focused on God, focused on others.

Rejecting the truth over and over again until it becomes nonexistent takes a lot of time and a lot of purposeful rejection. It is typically not one giant leap into the abyss. Most people would not purposefully drive the car into the ditch with one quick jerk of the wheel, but oh how we let ourselves drift—one small step, one intentional bad decision, one compromise after another. It is much like when a child wades in the ocean with a drifting current. He is splashing, playing, and jumping through the waves, when eventually he looks up and realizes that he has drifted far away from where he had started, unintentionally, but far away, nonetheless. As Screwtape reminds us, "Indeed the safest road to Hell is the gradual one—the gentle slope, soft underfoot, without sudden turnings, without milestones, without signpost."[4] This is a scary scenario. If it took a man going to a séance and selling his soul to the devil, most would avoid the eventual outcome. But a lifetime of suppressing the truth, rejecting that small voice of reason so long that it eventually disappears, is a much more likely road to find oneself on. Eventually the purposeful rejection of truth becomes less purposeful and more of just who we are. It becomes a part of our character.

Paul says that eventually God will give you over to it.[5] He says suppressing the truth will eventually lead, slowly but surely, to God taking his hands off the wheel and letting you steer. Via his characterization of George MacDonald in *The Great Divorce*, Lewis declares, "There are only two kinds of people in the end: those who say to God, "Thy will be done," and those to whom God says, "Thy will be done."[6] Even the prodigal son

---

4. Lewis, *Screwtape Letters*, 61.

5. Rom 1:18–32.

6. Lewis, *Great Divorce*, 75.

had to take several small steps away from his home before he reached his land of debauchery.[7]

I have seen this play out in my life multiple times. I never intentionally took one giant leap away from God, but I have often found myself taking gradual steps in the wrong direction. In my early high school years, I was living for God the best I knew how. I was a good kid overall, but the lure of this world really damaged my spiritual journey. I compromised once, then again, and then again. Eventually I was no longer compromising. It was just who I was, and it stuck with me for a very long time. It was during this time that I developed some struggles that I would battle for much of my adult Christian walk. The most devastating of all of these struggles? The one habit I developed that set me on a course of destruction? It was being ashamed of myself to the point that I could not bring my mistakes to God in repentance.

I would compromise. I would look at myself in the mirror. I would become disgusted over my actions. I would become disgusted at the unfamiliar dragon staring back at me. Yet instead of dealing with my mistakes boldly and quickly, or repenting my mistakes when I first realized them, I'd put them to the side. I'd feel embarrassed. I'd convince myself I would go to God later. For the time being, it was easier not to think about the darkness that had been revealed inside of me. This one devastating habit I developed, this one of repentance-avoidance, was more injurious to my soul than all of the parties and alcohol I could ever partake in and has moved me further away from God than any of the big, sexy sins that our culture more prevalently focuses on. Repentance avoidance is much more spiritually fatal than any high school party ever has been.

Whoever the author of Hebrews is says that we should approach the throne of grace with confidence.[8] Some translations say boldly. I think this was because of the damage that lingering sin in the Christian life can produce. Repentance was always embarrassing for me, especially at a younger age. I did not like the dual nature I saw creeping up. I did not like how easy it was for me to see the right thing to do and to see the wrong thing to do, and clearly choose the wrong one.

It was here, when I first began to notice the dual nature inside, that I first started to develop my low spiritual self-esteem. It was not pride, but embarrassment. I did not want to go to God in repentance because I did not want to deal with the darkness inside of me. I felt dirty that it was there, so it was best not to think about it. I think the less time it takes for Christians to realize that they really are two people, with two competing natures, and the

7. Luke 15: 11–32.
8. Heb 4:16.

nasty nature is going to rear its head from time to time, the quicker they can begin to start to enjoy the redemption that the cross of Christ offers them. Christians like me often do too much sulking and repentance avoidance and not nearly enough basking in the enjoyment of that redemption.

I never took the time to realize, however, that this repentance avoidance was nothing unique to me, but was in fact a scheme of the enemy: a scheme launched to intentionally move me one step further from God. *The Screwtape Letters* helped illuminate this for me, the way we used illumination in combat.

In the Marine Corps, I was part of a mortar squad. During combat, besides sending down steel rain on any number of targets if need be, part of our responsibility was to provide support to whatever Marines were patrolling in our area (if we ourselves were not the ones out patrolling, in which case we would have a team of mortar squads supporting us). Patrols often took place at nighttime and if a Marine saw any mischief that he thought could be the enemy working and scheming, he would call for illumination from the mortar squads. The mortar rounds would fire off and quickly illuminate the dark sky with a beautiful fire of green and white, floating down to the earth below attached to parachutes. Eventually they'd burn away, and rejoin the darkness, and we would fire more illumination rounds if need be. Sometimes this illumination would simply reveal some young boys herding goats or collecting sticks, and the Marines would allow the light to die out and move on. Sometimes the illumination would reveal an enemy who was making great ground under the cover of night, and the Marines would take care of it. Illuminating the enemy is always the first step in weeding him out. If one does not know where the enemy is working, the enemy is far more likely to make ground. If Christ followers do not understand the traps that their spiritual enemy is laying in front of them, they are far more likely to fall into them without notice or warning.

Lewis is a master at illumination. He is a master at exposing the enemy for who he really is. That is the whole concept of *The Screwtape Letters*. Throughout each letter of this classic book, Lewis shines bright illumination on an enemy making ground on the progress of a Christian . . . or at least trying to. When I read it the first time, like many others, I was stricken. It was profound. It almost seemed like Lewis really did discover a series of letters, written from one demon to the next. Every letter shined a more truthful light on the schemes of our spiritual enemy. Just like flipping on the kitchen light causes a cockroach to flee, shining a light on the enemy working in the life of a Christian often produces the same outcome. *The Screwtape Letters* does just that. I highly recommend it.

In one of these letters written by Screwtape to his younger protégé, Wormwood, the senior demon encourages his young trainee to keep his patient feeling remorseful over failures, yet never bold enough to go to God in repentance. Screwtape suggested that Wormwood allow his "patient" to wallow in his misery. He suggested that the "little brute" is allowed to feel like an abysmal failure but never act on his feeling like a failure. Wallowing in low spiritual self-esteem for his spiritual failures is perfectly OK with Screwtape. Let him do it! But do not let him act on it. Because, as Screwtape schemes, "the more often he feels without acting, the less he will be able ever to act, and in the long run, the less he will be able to feel." [9] The more the patient feels remorse but does not act on that remorse (i.e., repent), the less he will ever be able to act. Over time, these small steps of mistakes without repentance, the feeling of remorse that would have moved the patient towards repentance in the first place will slowly disappear. When remorse is gone, we've surrendered the biggest weapon God gave us to fight the enemy. This is a bad place to be in. Imagine if the drifting child on the beach eventually lost the ability to even know he or she was drifting.

I remember reading this letter of Screwtape for the first time. I cracked my neck and my fingers out of frustration. I actually became quite mad. I began to see the ground I had given to the enemy. The greatest temptation that the enemy of our soul will ever lay before us will never be sex, alcohol, drugs, power, or money. The greatest temptation will always be the temptation not to bring our mistakes to the cross of Christ for forgiveness. Lewis had nailed one of his schemes that I had fallen for for years. He illuminated the enemy's exact pattern in my life.

Looking back, it appears that this pattern of repentance avoidance has reared its head in my life mostly during times of great business, where all the demands of work, school, and being a single dad collide. I can describe the attack perfectly, like I have a page from the enemy's playbook: I will unknowingly let my spiritual guard down. I will give the enemy a foothold, and before you know it, I will stumble and fall. I will give in to a temptation I did not even realize was crouching at my door or make a mistake I did not see coming. At first, I will feel remorseful and promise myself that this time is the last . . . but instead of falling down in complete surrender and repentance, I will decide to manhandle it. *Next time! I've got this! I am capable. I am strong. I am even in professional ministry. Next time does not*

9. Lewis, *Screwtape Letters*, 66–67.

stand a chance. I can be much more moral than this . . . Then I move on, never in complete repentance, never in complete surrender, able to feel remorse less and less, adding layer upon layer of new dragon skin between my heart and the God who longs to heal it . . . Screwtape's exact schemes playing out in real time in my life: "Let the remorseful Christian think, but not act!" Let him feel sorrow for his sins but never to the point of turning everything over to God. Let him know that there is something wrong, something broken, but push off giving complete surrender to God, never letting him claw it out of his life. It is a road of destruction, with no signposts, a road of rejecting God time and time again until there was barely a God to reject. I eventually stopped that nonsense for the most part. I learned to boldly and quickly approach the throne of grace. I saw the opportunity to do so as a gift to embrace, not a shame to put off. It it literally over Christ's dead body that he offers us the chance to boldly approach God in repentance. If we're too small to do that, it's on us.

~

Eustace the Dragon wants the skin removed. He does not like what the darkness in his heart causes the reflection in water to show. He is tired of the battle. He is tired of life as a dragon. He longs to be a boy again. One day he finds himself giving up on a beach, hopeless and distraught . . . that is until he sees Aslan the Great Lion walking towards him, brightly illuminating the darkness with each step of his paw. Aslan is on the move. Eustace is scared of this lion at first, though he is not scared that the lion will eat him or attack him. He is simply afraid. Nevertheless, the Great Lion approaches.

Without words, Aslan has Eustace follow him deep into the mountains where they come upon a pool surrounded by beautiful fruit trees. This pool is appealing. It looks so very cooling. The dragon desperately wants to crawl inside the pool, especially given the pain in his arm that he knows the water will heal. Yet the Lion tells him, with or without the use of any words, that he will have to undress first. So, just like any self-confident strong man would do, he decides to claw at his own skin. *He can do it! He just needs to believe in himself! He has what it takes to overcome the scales draped across his body* . . . and eventually he does just that. The scales begin to come off.

He is successful at completely removing his own skin, and he tosses it to the ground in victory. It feels good, we are told. All that motivation and self-determination has paid off. Yet, unfortunately, Eustace looks down and to his horror he realizes that the skin remains. He is still a dragon. Although he feels wonderful at his attempts and probably feels like a strong, competent man, in the end he has in fact made no progress. I wonder if Eustace thinks to himself, *Next time! . . . I've got this! . . . I am capable! . . . There is more in me! . . . I am strong!* He must have thought something along those lines because he tries again and again, yet he keeps producing the same results.

Aslan must feel sorry for Eustace as he watches him struggle again and again to remove his own skin. It must have been a sad sight to see, especially for the Great Lion who cares so much for this son of Adam. At the same time, I am sure that Eustace is sincere in his attempts to rid himself of this awful condition—but sincerity rarely produces real change. Aslan could have allowed Eustace to struggle to remove his skin for a long time, day after day, year after year. Finally, the Great Lion speaks:

"You will have to let me undress you."[10]

This sounds awful to Eustace. He is much more comfortable giving it his best shot. Yet, he must realize that surrendering it all to Aslan is the only way out of the oppressing skin. Although he is afraid of the mighty claws he sees before him, he lays on his back in complete surrender, and allows the Lion to violently remove his skin. The pain is great, much more than he has ever experienced in his life, but Eustace stays on the ground and focuses on the pleasure of knowing it was finally being removed; eventually, the whole skin comes off.

Then Eustace, back in his old boyish skin, bathes in the refreshing pool. The pain is gone. The dragon skin lays on the ground in shreds. Eustace is new. He is restored. He has new clothes on . . . all because he stopped trying to remove the skin himself and allowed Aslan the Great Lion to tear it off.

I wonder how many people hold tight to their life simply out of fear what Christ will do. How many people hold on to their vices of choice simply because they are afraid of what full surrender looks like? How many Christians want the things of God, but not a full-scale renovation like they know they will receive if they were to lay down in complete surrender? In *Mere Christianity* Lewis writes, "Christ says 'Give me All. I don't want so much of your time and so much of your money and so much of your work: I want You. I have not come to torment your natural self, but to kill it . . . I will give you a new self instead. In fact, I will give you Myself: my own will shall become yours."[11]

It makes sense why trying to fix ourselves always seems so appealing. Eustace enjoys taking off his own skin. It was not painful at all, in fact, it felt good. Reading the right books; listening to the right motivating,

10. Lewis, *Voyage of Dawn*, 108.
11. Lewis, *Mere Christianity*, 105.

you-can-do-it preaching; attending the right break-out sessions; taking charge of our own change: this all sounds very desirable because *I am still in control*. When one is in charge of one's own transformation, the ball is still in their court. Maintaining control of one's life, even maintaining control over one's own change and moral improvement, is much more appealing than surrendering to someone else's control. It is safer. It does not have claws. It leaves the subject safely in the driver's seat . . . it leaves them precisely in the predicament that brought about devastation in the first place.

Dietrich Bonhoeffer writes, "When Christ calls a man, he bids him come and die."[12] This is a demand that Eustace and we are all afraid of following from time to time. Full surrender is the scariest of all of God's commands. Handing over the steering wheel to another is always cause for concern, especially if we're used to bad drivers. But God demands it all.

Much of my spiritual journey I have struggled with Christ because of my deep desire to keep my own change under my control—to hold on to the shore of all things temporal—even my own moralism. As a completely surrendered Christian, I needed to realize that change has nothing to do with trying harder, but everything to do with surrendering my will to Christ. It has everything to do with laying down and allowing him to undress me, as painful and as scary as that may be. No wonder moralism and a lack of complete surrender have contributed to my low spiritual self-esteem. The burden is still on me to change, and it has not worked. A remedy Lewis taught me was to learn to look past the claws and see the refreshing pool that awaits—to not even give the dragon skin a chance to accumulate by going to the throne of grace quickly, boldly, and daily. I think this may be what full surrender looks like. Doing this daily, though, requires me to be honest with who I am.

Christ says if your eye causes you to sin, then to gouge it out.[13] Imagine the pain of sticking one's finger behind the eye, clawing and gouging until it comes out. It would be quite painful. Is Christ being hyperbolic? Perhaps, but hyperbolic for what? I believe it is the seriousness we need to take the darkness in our own life, how drastically he longs for us to surrender to him, allowing him to remove the dragon skin, not ourselves, no matter the painful cost. No wonder the claws look scary to Eustace. Christ does not simply want to make a few moral adjustments. He wants to dig his claws in. He wants to rebuild the house. He wants the surrendered soul to walk away drastically different, forgiven, and rebuilt. Removing the dragon skin means laying down in full surrender. It means accepting the fact that we're

---

12. Bonhoeffer, *Discipleship*, 89.

13. Matt 5:29.

flawed and handing those flaws to God in repentance. It means searching our hearts for the bits that we are still keeping for ourselves . . . especially the parts we are keeping for ourselves. It means not beating ourselves up for the dual nature inside of us, but not excusing it either and engaging in repentance avoidance. Removing the dragon skin means coming to terms that our foolish, can-do attitudes will not suffice. Removing the dragon skin is good because it does not depend on us. Removing the dragon skin is scary because it does not depend on us. It depends on laying down our pride and our own ability. It depends on giving up the sham that we have our lives together. Indeed, we do not. It depends on Aslan the Great removing the skin for us.

7

Removing Our Illusions

When you go to a doctor you show him the bit of you that is wrong—say, a broken arm. It would be a mere waste of time to keep on explaining that your legs and eyes and throat are all right.

—C. S. Lewis, "On Forgiveness"[1]

A LARGE part of curing a battered spirit came from taking an honest look daily and making a truthful diagnosis of where I was on my spiritual journey . . . not where I wanted to be. Lewis brought this to the front of my mind. He writes, "We must lay before Him what is in us, not what ought to be in us."[2] He writes in "On Forgiveness" that with sin, there are no excuses. If there were excuses for our sins then forgiveness would not be mercy. It would simply be justice. If there are any excuses, God will be the excuser. All that remains after the excuses, the self-centeredness, the meanness, the unrelenting pride, the nastiness, the darkest parts of our soul . . . that's what we must find, come to terms with, and lay before God. It is the *real* ailments that the doctor is interested in. If we are sick, let us confess our symptoms, not all the ways we are feeling well. Being completely honest with the Great Physician and with ourselves is the best way to root out disease.

There is much freedom in seeing oneself as one really is and bringing that to God. It softens the shock that comes about, and the low-esteem that

1. Lewis, "On Forgiveness," 180.
2. Lewis, *Letters to Malcom*, 22.

accumulates, when one falls into a spiritual mistake. This, of course, does not mean we accept the darkness inside, contently living in heavy-handed disobedience; we must remember to be found in the resistance. But our mistakes are to be brought before God: honest, naked, and sincere, trusting that what Christ did on the cross was sufficient to cover those iniquities. The fact that our soul cries out for perfection only means that there is perfection out there, and we will one day have it—though not on this side of eternity. So, in the meantime we need to remove any illusion of ourselves that is causing us harm.

Lewis is an example to me in this area. He was extremely comfortable in his own skin and comfortable that God loved him despite his flawed soul. He helped me come to terms with the depraved man that I really am and not the perfect man I told myself I should be. He writes, "To confess our sins before God is certainly to tell Him what He knows much better than we."[3] Learning to accept these hard truths about myself was like coming out of the water after a ship wreck. I could breathe. I was still swimming in the middle of an ocean, desperate and in need of a lifeboat, but I could breathe nonetheless, and it felt good. I knew I could survive. I had to learn that my sinful humanity did not surprise God and it should not surprise me. God remembers I am made from dirt.[4] I need to remember that too.

Being honest with who we are and where we are, and not trying to be something we are not, can be scary, but it is so redeeming if we can get to that place. In land navigation, it would do no good to place myself closer than I really was to the endpoint on a map just because I did not like where I would've had to plot myself. It does no good pretending we are more spiritual, more moral, more clean than we actually are. That gives God nowhere to work.

We're often afraid . . . afraid of the darkness within . . . afraid that we're not really the person we portray to everyone else. I suppose we do not want to take an honest look at where we are because, ultimately, we're too afraid of how far from God we really are—forgetting that Christ has made up that gap, no matter the distance.

The good news is that, while the road to hell is soft and gradual, with no real signposts, the road back to God does not have to be. Long distances of travel in the wrong direction can be erased with a simple 180-degree turn. The prodigal son simply had to make the decision to come home. While he may have taken a thousand steps in the wrong direction, all it took was one step back to start the journey home, and the Father ran to him. Lewis

3. Lewis, *Letters to Malcom*, 20.

4. Ps 103:14.

reminds me that one turn, one sincere moment of repentance can change it all. He writes, "One wrench and the tooth will be out. You can begin as if nothing had ever gone wrong. White as snow."[5]

One of my favorite portraits Lewis ever illustrated of what happens once one is completely honest with the darkness inside and fully surrenders to God is found in *The Great Divorce*. This tale of a group of tourists from hell who take a bus ride to heaven would be whimsical if it was not so sad and unnervingly realistic. Just about every one of these "ghosts" from hell find excuses why they will not fully surrender to God and remain in the freedom of heaven. They feel better than the poor souls in heaven, duped by a tyrannical God who demanded that they conform. One by one we read them refusing to be honest with themselves, rejecting the truth that is so evidently right in front of their face, and one by one we see them getting back on the bus, awaiting their trip back to hell. There is a ghost, however, that chose a different scenario.

We are introduced to a ghost unlike any of the others in the story. This ghost has a stowaway passenger on his shoulder—a little red, tail-twitching lizard that routinely whispers unknown statements into the chauffer's ear. As the ghost is limping along, away from the westward mountains of heaven, he is stopped by what we are led to believe is a bright and burning angel. The ghost has very little time for the angel, however. He lets the angel know that he is grateful for the hospitality, but he has to be off because the little chap on his shoulder will not be quiet like he had previously promised to be. The angel politely and calmly asks if the ghost would like him to silence and kill the snarling lizard, but the ghost will have none of it. He deflects the question. Yet this does not stop the persistent angel. He asks him the question again, "Don't you want him killed?" It eventually becomes tempting to the ghost, but the little devil on his shoulder gives him ample excuses why this angel is not to be trusted.

Over the next few pages readers witness the all-too-familiar struggle of someone that wants to let go and submit themselves to God but refuses to be honest with the deplorable demons on their shoulder, continuing to justify the little critters. When one does not recognize the blatant darkness in their life and take an honest look at the person allowing that darkness to remain, it will be impossible to ever take the next step. One does not have to cure the darkness on their own. But one does have to recognize it.

5. Lewis, *Great Divorce*, 38.

The angel asks a total of ten times if the ghost would like the sinful little lizard killed (we are led to believe represents lust in the ghost's life), all to no avail. Yet the angel slowly approaches the two, hands out, ready to rid the ghost of this pesky, twitching creature. The ghost continues to argue and find a series of reasons as to why the sin should not be removed. He even offers the angel the possibility of a slow, gradual removal of the lizard. To this, the angel responds, "The gradual process is of no use at all."

The ghost is not being honest with the gravity of the situation. He suggests that perhaps they will deal with the lizard another day, to which the angel replies, "There is no other day."

The ghost is afraid of the pain that might come with the removal of the lizard. To this, the angel assures, "I never said it wouldn't hurt you. I said it wouldn't kill you."

The back and forth continues as the angel creeps nearer by. "I cannot kill it against your will. It is impossible. Have I your permission?"

The trembling ghost wants the lizard gone, but is too afraid of the pain, the process, and the potential chance of death.

I imagine the ghost can see over the shoulders of the angel. I imagine he can see the westward mountains where he would be free to live, free of his afflictions, free of the dreary town below. He is surrounded by love, by paradise, and somewhere deep in those mountains is his true longing, his true passion, his Creator. Yet, in that moment, his world is too small, and he is unable to see the situation before him. The small whispers of the lizard seem to make more sense than a complete surrender of his will. The whispers seem rational and enticing. The angel, much like the claws of Aslan appeared to Eustace, seems frightening, dangerous, and unfamiliar, suspicious even. Like many, the ghost desires beauty and freedom but finds too many reasons to hold on to the small, comfortable world that he knows all too well.

Eventually, however, the ghost gives in. Against his own will, against his own flawed reasoning, and certainly against the wishes of the lizard and the lizard's father below, he surrenders. He stops pushing it off. He stops rationalizing. He is honest. He gives in.

"'Damn and blast you! Go on, can't you? Get it over. Do what you like,' bellowed the Ghost, but ended, whimpering, 'God help me. God help me.'"[6]

The angel spares not a second. He grabs the lizard, breaks his back, and throws him to the ground, repelling the screaming ghost backwards in agony.

6. Lewis, *Great Divorce*, 110.

What happens next gives me chills and even a bit of moisture in the corner of eyes. I imagine myself clinging to my sins of choice in the past, knowing that joy and freedom are just beyond the horizon . . . all the while rejecting the truth about my humanity and finding every reason I can summon to return back to them, never being honest with myself that they were really there. They are lying, crooked lizards on my back, but they are safe, and they are familiar. I find comfort in them in some strange way. I am scared of the burning angel in front of me. The claws of the Great Lion are horrifying. What would life look like on the other side of those claws, free from the whispers and the lies of the enemy? Lewis knows the answer.

He writes that the ghost grows. He grows much larger, much stronger, and more solid than he had been before. He grows solid hands and legs. A solid head materializes. He grows to become not much smaller than the angel. At the same time, the lizard grows. He still twitches and shudders on the ground. He grows bigger. His tail grows longer and morphs into a collection of beautiful, flowing hair. The lizard stands up to become a beautiful stallion, more glorious than the narrator has ever seen. The new solid man grasps the horse by the neck, pulls the stallion in close, and they breathe into each other's nostrils. What was once the pale ghost's biggest burden has now become the solid man's favorite asset and new companion.

The new-made man turns from the horse and flings himself to the ground, embracing the feet of the burning one. He then begins to cry liquid tears that, in this country, are indistinguishable from liquid love and brightness. They are one and the same. Then, as quickly as he had fallen to the ground, he stands, and climbs aboard his stallion. He gives the angel a wave goodbye, kicks his heels against the horse, and the two dash towards the mountains to continue their journey of going further up and further in.[7] All of nature, the trees, the hills, and the waters sing a beautiful tune as a newly-made, solid man rides toward the hills, renewed, forgiven, and restored. Beautiful . . . suppose God has great beauty for us, just on the other side of our honesty and full surrender of ourselves?

I relate greatly to this ghost. Most of my adult Christian life, I have let the little lizards remain on my back, telling me lie after lie about why I should not surrender every situation and all that I am to Christ and trust him with the results on the other side of the claws. Lewis is instrumental in shining a light on this behavior I have carried for far too long. How healing it is to expose it and remove it from my repertoire. For the Christian, coming to God as he or she really is, not how they wish to be, is crucial for any chance of spiritual healing to take place—and why not? Christ died for

7. Lewis, *Great Divorce*, 110–12.

sinfully-flawed humanity just the way they were: dirty, broken enemies of God. Why do we think if we are currently dirty, broken enemies of God, he will have nothing to do with us? Indeed, it is over his dead body that he accepts us as such.

I like Lewis's analogy of the lizard because it is specific. This ghost does not seem to have a vast chasm that is separating him from God. He only has one particular element that he is clinging too. There is one roadblock in between him and infinite fulfillment, and by no coincidence, it is the hardest one to give up. The pain of having the lizard removed is something that the ghost has never experienced, but the beauty that awaits him on the other side of surrender is also something that he has never experienced. Although we are currently still living in the land of the lizards, we do not have the luxury (quite yet) of riding away into the mountains, all would-be mistakes behind us. But we are free to recognize the lizards as they are and deal with them appropriately. The moment we surrender and allow the burning one to destroy a lizard, another one will creep up. We must take this as it is: another attack, but another chance at surrender. We'll have some sort of lizard on our shoulders until our last days in this life. It will be in the next when we are finally able to fully enjoy an existence unblemished by our ever-present ability to give in to the worst parts about ourselves. We may indeed have some sort of lizard on our shoulder throughout our whole life. That's to be expected. What's not to be expected is its journey with us into the thereafter. Do not worry. It will not be allowed.

8

God Forgive God

*The conclusion I dread is not 'So there's no God after all,' but
'So this is what God's really like.' Deceive yourself no longer.*

—C. S. LEWIS, *A GRIEF OBSERVED*[1]

MY two brothers are easily the best friends I have ever had. We have
been through a lot together . . . some extreme ups and downs. No
matter how well things were going or how trying the times became, we
never lost our sense of humor and never lost our love for one another. In
the midst of some pretty rough circumstances that would test any family's
strength, sometimes our biggest priority was just to make one another
laugh. My most cherished memories I have in my memory bank all include growing up with my two brothers.

My oldest brother Caleb was a beacon in my life. He loved so well.
He had his shortcomings for sure and struggled with a short fuse at times,
but he loved so well. He had countless friends from all walks of life. While
he struggled like me to find his place in mainstream Christian culture, his
faith in Christ was as solid as it comes. In fact, he followed Christ's example
more than anyone I have ever known. His best friends were made up of
both Christians and those that many religious people have traditionally
been prone to hold at an arm's distance: atheists, homosexuals, spiritual-
ists, questioners, and just those who struggle to find a place of belonging
behind the walls of a church. On a side note, I always found it interesting

1. Lewis, *Grief Observed*, 6–7.

73

that when a Christian is welcoming to those our Christian culture struggles to accept, that Christian stands out. Should that not be the norm? The mere fact that those who maintain relationships with the marginalized is worth mentioning is curious and should give us pause to look inward. If we all followed the example of Jesus, would our lives not help but intersect with the marginalized? Would we not all surround ourselves with criminals, prostitutes, and the equivalent of modern-day tax collectors? Not only would our churches be welcoming to them (as I know that many are today), but we would be going to them. We'd be going to them to invite them, not only into our churches, but into our lives. Indeed, the bulk of our relationships would be with the marginalized, the outcast, the despised, and the broken.

Anyway, back to my brother. My brother was welcoming to all, no matter who they were. He was certainly welcoming to me. He knew all of my shortcomings, both superficial and hidden deep below, yet he loved me deeply and consistently. I have many fond memories of my brother stepping up to prove his love for me both in action and word.

Until around the third grade or so, I was what my speech therapist called "tongue-tied." I had tremendous trouble pronouncing basic words. One was able to understand Donald Duck easier than some of the gibberish that would spew out of my mouth. My favorite restaurant was "Baco Bell" for the first ten years of my life or so. Yet I have specific memories of Caleb getting into fist fights with kids in our neighborhoods on my behalf because they made fun of the way I talked (eighties bullies were the worst). He was a constant source of encouragement. He supported my music aspirations. He supported me when I was in the Marines—throughout boot camp, combat, and beyond. He even thought it was a great idea when I told him I wanted to be president one day . . . although I've slightly changed my aspirations since then.

When I was overseas in the Marine Corps and my family back home started to fall apart, he was my sleuth on the ground whenever I couldn't get ahold of my son. I would have to get up at ridiculous hours in the morning, use a satellite phone to call him, who was hot on the trail of trying to locate my son. He knew that if my mind was not right as a squad leader on the other side of the world, it was not going to be good for anyone I was supposed to be leading. He did the best that he could to ease my mind 7,249 miles away.

A cherished memory I have of my brother took place after I got home from that deployment. I was in pretty bad shape, emotionally. Out of all my deployments, this one was particularly rough. I had done everything in my power to rescue my family and keep my boy's parents together. There was one night, though, that I knew I was going to be unsuccessful. There was a night when the realization came crashing that I was going to be a single father, and the solid family foundation both he and his mom had wanted to give to him was never going to be delivered. I was a broken Marine; weary from deployments while simultaneously trying to rescue my family. I was at my lowest point of my life. We were both equally flawed and young and made poor choices, but neither of us wanted to split up what we had given our boy. Nevertheless, the writing was on the wall. I was devastated. It was a dark night, literally and figuratively. Naturally, I fell back on my brother Caleb.

I was sitting in an empty house with no furniture or even dishes, about an hour and a half away from my brother at the time. I called him. I knew he couldn't fix it, but I wanted to bring him into my pain. I broke down immediately. He heard the brokenness in my voice. When you have the deep love for one another that Christ asks that you have, and you hear a deep brokenness in a brother's voice, you don't make excuses. You get in your car and go to him. Caleb did that for me late that night. He grabbed his guitar and a bottle of whiskey, and he was on the road.

He found me sitting on an empty porch in downtown Oklahoma City, attempting to choke down one of my wife's cigarettes. I didn't even smoke. He walked up, sat down beside me, and started to strum his guitar. We both sat on the porch and sipped whiskey out of the bottle as he played and sang to me. He sang worship songs. He sang Johnny Cash and some of my favorite punk band's acoustic stuff. He tried to sing songs that fit the pain that I was experiencing. He didn't say anything or try and fix it. He didn't tell me everything was going to be ok. He allowed me to sit there and be broken. It meant the world to me. Yes, the whiskey was an immediate and temporary escape, and I don't recommend that one nurse their problems in that way, but that night did more for me than anyone telling me that God had a plan and this was all for a reason, or giving me a Bible verse or a pre-concocted nugget of wisdom. I just wanted to be broken next to someone I loved. My brother knew that, and he just let his tears fall with my tears, without trying to fix a thing. I hold many memories of my brother near and dear to my heart. That one was special. I praise God for allowing me to have that night with Caleb. Caleb was a beacon in my life.

So naturally, when I received a phone call around 3:00 a.m. that Caleb's heart had stopped, it was the equivalent of someone waking me up to tell me they're going to be removing a couple of limbs from my body . . . actually, it was worse than that. I would gladly trade a couple limbs to have Caleb back. Enter a new sensation that I had never experienced before: intense anger at God.

I simply did not understand. My brother did not die because he was out drinking and driving. He didn't die because some idiot was texting on the highway. Caleb didn't pass away after years of smoking or boozing or being an avid rock climber. God just turned his heart off. He was young. He was happy and he was healthy. He and his wife had dinner in my apartment, went home, and went to sleep. God chose to turn his heart off while he was sleeping.

Cognitively I knew that bad things happen to good people, but I always thought there was a reason why. I always thought that if one stepped back, one was able to see the silver lining. God's fingerprints would be evident. Here, there was no silver lining from my perspective, and seemingly, none from God's either. It was pretty much just pure thievery. My brother was a great guy. His wife was pregnant with their second baby, and he had just landed his dream job in upstate New York where he would work with autistic kids, something he had studied for years to do. He was already packed. In fact, that's why they were having dinner at my apartment, because they would be leaving soon. He had his dream job, with his dream family, and for the very first time in his life, he felt extremely happy and purposeful. Then God said, "Nope!" and he decided to flip the switch and turn my brother's heart off. I was angry at God to say the least. *Thanks for that one, all-loving God!*

But here was my dilemma. I was always taught to never be angry with God. I was always told that he has a plan and a purpose. The minute tragedy would strike, there was always someone there to make excuses for God. *He knew what he was doing. We can't see the forest for the trees. Trust him in the pain, in the midst of nonsense. Trust him during the times that it appears that no one is behind the wheel up there. Trust him even more. Do not be angry towards God. He has this!*

This was engrained in me and my Christian culture so much that it scared me that I was angry at God. I thought this was a step away from God. I thought I was giving up my faith because how could I be angry with God and trust him at the same time? Heck, I was going to go into professional ministry at this point! No way was I allowed to let people know I firmly disagreed with a decision God had made. I was infuriated with God, but at the same time I was tremendously frightened about that fury. This was just a new sensation that the third-stringer Christian had never encountered before. I'm sure if I was a first-stringer, I would be able to see God's purpose in this whole thing. But I could not. This was again a reminder that I was on the outside. I was not where God wanted to me to be. I could not see the meaning behind it all—I dared someone try and tell me.

I remember the morning after my brother had passed. I had spent the whole evening mourning and crying. I didn't sleep a bit. I was wide awake and just sat in a quiet apartment wondering how I should be feeling. My girlfriend at the time came over to be a part of the mourning process. She did great in that moment. She just sat there in the quiet and allowed me to be damaged. She felt no need to fix my problem either; that's all I could have asked for.

Frozen with grief. Frozen with shock. I was having some of the strongest feelings I have ever felt, yet no feelings at all. I was having the emotional equivalent of when a body goes into shock. I do remember that the lines on my face were that of an angry man, not a sad man. I was angry, yet frozen.

In the silence of the moment I looked down at the mess of books scattered about my desk. I was about a year into my Lewis Remedy, although I did not recognize it as any sort of remedy or project at the time. I had my "to read" stack surrounded by a disheveled pile of recently highlighted and marked-up "have read" books by C. S. Lewis. At this point I was slightly familiar with his biography. I knew he had lost a wife late in his life. I knew he journaled about it, and I knew he did it under a pseudonym. I scanned the titles in the "to read" stack and grabbed A Grief Observed. Of course, this copy had C. S. Lewis written on the spine, not N. W. Clerk, the name Lewis originally released it under. I picked it up. Numb with pain. Frozen with anger. I read these words:

No one ever told me that grief felt so like fear.[2]

That was exactly what I felt in that moment. Fear. My fear was masquerading as grief and anger, but it was fear, nonetheless. When Lewis lost his mom, he described it as the great continent sinking. Everything else in his life was sea and islands. In my scattered life, my brothers were my continents. They were my consistency. They were the unmovable grounds I could always retreat to . . . and now a great one had fallen. It felt like fear: fear that I would have to do life without my brother from now on; fear of what would happen to my family; fear that something like this was allowed to happen; fear that no one was seeming at the helm of this crazy existence.

Over the next couple hours, I devoured this short four-chapter book. My girlfriend was kind enough to sit in my living room, literally watching me read in silence. For the next several weeks, this would be my life: silence, fear, and reading. Eventually, any healing that would take place would be done so by outside intervention and conversations with people who loved me and cared about me, but for now, the lazy, selfish, introverted side of me

2. Lewis, *Grief Observed*, 1.

wanted nothing to do with the outside world. I instantly found a grieving partner. I was thrilled to have made his acquaintance for such a time as this.

Lewis was not immediately comforted by his faith in Christ upon losing his wife, and something dark in me enjoyed that. In fact, he was ready to outright reject anyone who tried to bring healing to his soul via a Bible verse or a cliché quote about everything having a purpose, etc. He writes that he had little patience with the common Christian responses. He writes, "It is hard to have patience with people who say, 'There is no death' or 'Death doesn't matter.' There is death. And whatever is matters."[3] I agreed. Death did matter. Death still matters. In the early stages of grief, it is very difficult to stomach someone who sees the big picture.

Lewis asks about God, "Why is He so present a commander in our time of prosperity and so very absent a help in time of trouble?"[4] Lewis even asks questions in his anguish that I didn't even know I was asking, until the moment I read it. What does it mean that his wife is now in God's hands? Is that supposed to be a comfort to him? Was she not in God's hands the whole time? Are God's hands gentler the moment we leave the body? And if so, why? If God's goodness is inconsistent with him hurting us, then either God does no good or he does not exist. In the only life that we do know, God has hurt us beyond all imagination, so why would we ever think that he would not do the same in the next life? "Sometimes it is hard not to say, 'God forgive God,'" Lewis writes. Because if our faith is true, God did not ever forgive God. He indeed crucified him.[5]

I am so thankful to Lewis for journaling these raw emotions. They are painful. They are uncomfortable. They are sacrilegious. But they are real.

I knew that Lewis eventually recovered from his wrestle with the Divine, but for the time being I was happy to throw a spiritual tantrum with my would-be, distant mentor. People gain much credibility when they drop the sham, when they drop the appearance of having the answers, and allow themselves to be real . . . even if real means raw, broken, and full of doubts. At this point in my journey, Lewis was no longer an author or a professor . . . he was a friend.

I think God enjoys us in our raw form. He seems to be confident enough in himself and in his identity to let us rattle off a few complaints his way. Too many people try to stand up for God when something is said that might hurt his feelings. I think God has a pretty good track record. At this point he has got to have a bit of thick skin. Scripture is littered with people

---

3. Lewis, *Grief Observed*, 15.

4. Lewis, *Grief Observed*, 6.

5. Lewis, *Grief Observed*, 27–28.

who love God, generally want to serve and follow him, yet do not agree with him along the way.

One of my favorite examples of raw emotion and anger towards God in the Bible is found in the story of Mary and Martha. In the narrative, we find Martha desperately trying to prepare dinner for Jesus and his many disciples. She has much work to do and feels she is all alone in doing it. Her significance is on the line, and she is sweating it. I know firsthand how much weight and value a first century Middle Eastern culture puts on a woman being a good host. It's true today. Martha is more than just OCD or a hard worker. Her worth and her value is on the line with a house full of men hoping for a good meal. Toss in the fact that one of these men is the Son of God, and you've got a recipe for a stressed-out Martha. All this stress and so much on the line, and where was her sister Mary? Chilling at the feet of Jesus.

On a side note, I think the modern person relates much more to Martha than Mary. In our fast-paced, workaholic, professional world, Marys have a hard time making it through any hiring process. I mean, we all love Jesus, but when it's time to work, it's time to work.

So, Martha loses it. What's her complaint? Is it towards Mary? No. Is it towards one of the dirty, bulky fishermen with their hairy feet up on Martha's coffee table? No. Her complaint is to Jesus. She cries, "Lord, don't you care?" She demands that Jesus answer her. She asks if he even cares that she is working so hard to get dinner prepared, the table set, and make everyone fat and happy, while Mary is just lounging in the living room with the fellas.

"Lord, don't you care?"

I've been there. More than once. *Lord, don't you care that this person is making up lies about me that are devastating to my career? Lord, don't you care that my son's family is falling apart? Lord, don't you care that I am losing the one job my son and I are dependent on for our survival? Lord, don't you care that my brother's wife is pregnant and now has to raise two children alone? Lord, don't you care that you took the only person that knows me fully and loves me anyway? Lord, don't you care?*

In today's world we are pummeled with reasons to ask, "Lord, don't you care?" I could list them all here, but the reader would quickly become depressed and put this book down. Just turn on the news. Scroll through social media. Read a statistic. Visit a marginalized community. Visit a Third World country. *Lord, don't you care?*

I'm glad this story is in the Bible. Jesus doesn't mind the question, by the way. He understands. Martha is not chastised or thrown out of the group. She is not stoned or accused of blasphemy. She is not told to confess her sins of anger or that she is in danger of the fires of hell. Jesus is strong. Jesus is secure. When someone is strong and secure in who they are and who God is, the strongest criticisms seem nothing more than minute, water-off-a-duck's-back statements that should be addressed in love. Jesus knows that this is much more about the questioner than the questioned.

Jesus simply says, "Martha, Martha," and proceeds to tell her that she is tired and worried about many things, but there is only one thing she should be worried about. She should only ever be concerned with doing exactly what Mary is doing. And what is Mary doing? She is at the feet of Jesus. She is simply enjoying God.

Dinner still has to be made. There are still at least thirteen hungry men who need to recharge and enjoy a meal, but while Martha is laboring away, why not pause for a minute to enjoy God?

Why not take a moment to make sure your worth and value are not on the line? Your worth and value come from one place only, and it is not in the kitchen. Why not realize that in the scheme of things, there is, in all actuality, nothing to be worked up about when Jesus is sitting in your living room? Yes, go to work, and do it with a sense of intentionality and excellence, but also doing it while enjoying your Savior. Relax.

Jesus embraces the complaints against him and uses it as a teachable moment. One of Lewis's great heroes, George MacDonald, writes, "Complaint against God is far nearer to God than indifference about him."[6] I concur. If we're questioning God, if we're wrestling against God, if we feel that we are letting God down, then let us take heart. Only in a relationship are struggles like this allowed to exist. No one struggles against the Tooth Fairy.

When Lazarus dies, his sister's first reaction is to blame Christ for being there. The Old Testament has countless examples of strong men of God who lose their confidence in their God's decision-making process: people like David, Jeremiah, and Moses. When it comes to putting these raw emotions in the Bible, I'm glad God didn't have a better public relations strategy. I'm glad he left the real, the raw, and the embarrassing. These biblical heroes may have been wrong in the moment and flawed in their interpretations of their anger, but at least they're real. God can work with real people much better than he can work with fake. With imperfect, real people, no matter how flawed, there's room for improvement. With people who have their act together, God doesn't have a lot of wiggle room.

6. Lewis, *George MacDonald*, 167.

That's why *A Grief Observed* is so important to me, so cherished during a time that I desperately needed something to cherish. This is because at times it really did seem like we had a God who, "Time after time, when He seemed most gracious He was really preparing the next torture."[7] It felt good to throw this tantrum and be mad at the God that I knew could have stopped this. It angered me more to think that he had that whole situation in the palm of his hand.

Anyone with any knowledge of C. S. Lewis's biography, especially that which takes place later in his life, knows the he does not remain in this state of anger towards God. In fact, by the time Lewis concludes *A Grief Observed*, he has calmed down, slowed his breathing, hung his head, and walked back to the God he had been throwing verbal bombs at. He felt he had been hit by God and his angry journaling was his only tool to hit back. He writes, "It was just Billingsgate—mere abuse; 'telling God what I thought of Him.' And of course, in all abusive language, 'what I thought' didn't mean what I thought true."[8] He knows the truth is that God is good, and yes, God does in fact have a plan. In what just was a beautifully constructed temper-tantrum, yet also a healthy exercise in countering his beliefs (one that we should all do from time to time), Lewis is acting out simply because he is hurt and wants to offend the God who hurt him, knowing full well that God can take it. He also admits that he wants to offend those worshippers who are so bulldoggishly ready to come to God's defense.[9] (That is probably my favorite part of the whole book.)

Ironically, Lewis's brief anger and public "hitting back" of God, expanded my view of God immensely. It was one more layer of petty religion that I was able to peel away from my view of the divine and see God not how others tell me how God is, but one step closer to seeing him as he really is. God can take it. And what's even better, God understands. He has experience with that whole "My God, why have you forsaken me?" thing.

What great faith it takes to experience tragedy and actually get upset with God over it, instead of abandoning one's faith or putting on a sham of understanding and agreement. How much more real and tangible does that relationship become? If a long-time married couple reflects back and realizes that they have never really had any actual conflict, never had any ups

---

7. Lewis, *Grief Observed*, 30.
8. Lewis, *Grief Observed*, 40.
9. Lewis, *Grief Observed*, 40.

and downs, or never questioned each other's decisions, they would come to the conclusion that one of them is either running a dictatorship where the other is not free to express any thoughts or feelings, or one of them is, in all actuality, a robot. Neither one is a shining example of a real relationship that others would aspire to have. As ironic as it sounds, learning to be mad at God, to disagree with his decisions yet remain in submission to him, has expanded my relationship with him by leaps and bounds. The honeymoon always ends when the first bit of disagreement arises—but that's when the real relationship begins.

In a culture where God is often crammed into a box, given his boundaries, told what pleases him and what does not, packaged, branded, given his logos and sold as is, it is therapeutic for me to read this spiritual powerhouse tell God, "I don't particularly care for you right now." It heals me a bit to know that God is much bigger than our small minds that are so quick to want to justify and protect God. Learning that it's OK to be mad at God takes the clean Jesus that has been sold to me for so long out of the hands of the sellers, making him more real and delivering him nearer to my hands and my heart.

Timothy Keller writes, "If you have a God great and transcendent enough to be mad at because he hasn't stopped evil and suffering in the world, then you have (at the same moment) a God great and transcendent enough to have good reasons for allowing it to continue that you can't know."[10] When it comes to losing my brother, and God's choice to take him away, I look for no good "reason." I'm not trying to trace God's fingerprints. I never have had any moment of revelation where I think, "And that's what God had planned all along!" It still hurts. I still do not understand. I am still incomplete without him, and do not have any plans of becoming complete. I have probably healed as much as I ever will. I have healed in some ways, but not in a complete way. I have healed, to use one of Lewis's example, not in the way someone heals from pneumonia or the flu but healed like that of someone who lost a limb. I just have to get used to my new handicap. I still disagree. I still want him back. Yet I am still drawn towards the One who took him from me. I will continue to hobble my way towards Aslan's Country.

Lewis lived in what seemed to be a constant awareness of eternity and the life that awaited him. One of the most attractive aspects of Lewis's theology

10. Keller, *Reason for God*, 25.

is how little regard he gives our current world, in my opinion. Our current existence is but the title page of the real story. We are living in what Lewis calls the Shadowlands. It's a blurry, cheap rip-off of the world we were meant for. The Shadowlands are the cover and title page of the real novel. It is quickly discarded for the actual story. I am quite confident that once he regained his spiritual composure after suffering through the death of Joy, his view on the afterlife was of the utmost comfort. He writes about his wife, whom he had named H. in *A Grief Observed*:

> "If H. 'is not,' then she never was. I mistook a cloud of atoms for a person."[11]

This was a great comfort for me while dealing with the loss of my brother. If my brother's death was the end of his existence, then it was all a farce anyway. Why would I be upset about the loss of a clump of atoms but for the selfish reasons those atoms brought me? If my brother was a person, then he still is a person, with his same quirks, same sense of humor, same warm heart, same short fuse. He is still a person who is moving ever-deeper into the mountains of God. Yes, I am sad and have been injured in a way that I will not heal from completely while I still live in the Shadowlands. If I am sad, I am sad for that reason alone. I am sad for what he meant to me and for others. I am sad that the world lost a strong asset. I am sad that it will be seventy years or so before his children get to meet him. But I will not be sad for my brother who stepped into eternity and found the joy that could not be satisfied on earth.

At the end of *The Chronicles of Narnia: The Last Battle*, after the Shadowlands are destroyed and the new Narnia is created, Jewel the Unicorn stomps his hoof, neighs, and cries:

> "I have come home at last! This is my real country! I belong here. This is the land I have been looking for all my life, though I never knew it till now . . . Come further up, come further in!"[12]

Coming home at last will be a welcomed event. The country that we have been searching for through endless endeavors will be presented before us, and it will all make sense. Though we will not know it until that point, complete union with our Creator has been what we were searching for all along. Yes, our friends and family that we lost along the way will be there, but that will just be the icing on the cake. Yes, we will reunite, and it will be beautiful. But the most beautiful thing that will come from our reunion

---

11. Lewis, *Grief Observed*, 28.
12. Lewis, *Last Battle*, 196.

will be the realization that we get to experience God together. We get to rest in our creation's purpose together. We get to go further up and further in together. I must say I look forward to that day with great anticipation.

One of the greatest achievements anyone can make in this life is to gain and maintain the ability to constantly keep one's eyes on the next life. Lewis achieved that. I achieve it from time to time but have to pull back and refocus every now and then to keep eternity, the real life and real world I was created for, in the forefront of my mind. In the moments that have brought me down the most—when I lost my brother, when my struggles with alcohol seemed hopeless, when I lost a job or the woman I loved—in all of those moments where I would be tempted and permitted to be mad at God, Lewis reminds me that these temporary problems are but a mere gnat in the grand scheme of things, a blip on the radar of our complete existence. I have to remind myself not to get caught up in the Shadowlands and the problems herein. They will soon be forgotten. We'll laugh one day when we look back at the pettiness that used to worry and bother us. The loss of a relationship, the loss of a job, the loss of money, even the loss of life will be but a punchline in the life to come, the real one, that was created especially for us.

I can't imagine what it would be like for our Savior to look at us with the deepest and most understanding eyes, simply saying "Martha, Martha." I can't imagine our Heart's Desire, one day, placing a hand on our shoulder, or perhaps behind our neck, repeating our name twice, and embracing us. That will be the most potent moment of our lives. We'll calm down. We'll stop the huffing and puffing. The wild beast will be tame. Like Reepicheep, the brave mouse at the end of *The Chronicles of Narnia: The Voyage of the Dawn Treader*, we will drop our unnecessary weapons and venture deep into Aslan's Country. Every little issue we ever had from our measly existence will fade away. Our petty political differences will be no more. Our petty relational problems will evaporate. Our petty financial, spiritual, racial, and sexual squabbles will dissolve . . . all because our Creator places his hand on us and repeats our name twice. We are so worried, so bothered, so stressed about so many things. However, there is only one thing that we need.

9

Canceled Handwriting

*"Jesus has cancelled the handwriting which was against us.
Lift up our hearts!"*

—C. S. LEWIS, A LETTER WRITTEN TO LEWIS'S FRIEND,
DON GIOVANNI CALABRIA[1]

L EWIS wrote the preceding words to his friend, Don Giovanni Calabria, in December 1951. Calabria was an Italian Roman Catholic
Priest who was known for the great piety and somberness found in his
writings. He was also engaged in community development and had
opened an orphanage in his hometown of Verona. Lewis wanted to remind his friend not to get caught up in his own mistakes. He reminded
him about how much he writes about his own sins and shortcomings.
Lewis warranted his friend to lift up his heart, lest his humility should
pass over into anxiety or sadness. Out of all the commands that God has
bestowed upon the believer, the command to "rejoice and always rejoice"
carries just as much weight as the ones we fumble with day in and day
out. Not only is God concerned with our character, he is also concerned
that we rejoice along the way.

Lewis may have written these words, originally in Latin, to his friend,
but he might as well have been writing it to all of us. This is the recurring
cycle we deal with: there are known flaws in our lives that lead us to humility, which is healthy, but when there is so much self-loathing that it gives way

1. Lewis, *Yours, Jack,* 173.

85

to sadness and less-than feelings, it become unhealthy and makes it hard for us to enjoy God. Lewis here is referencing Saint Paul when he writes that his friend should rejoice.[2] If Paul, the writer of much of the New Testament, reminds his readers to rejoice, despite the failures and shortcomings in their lives, then we would be advised to listen to those words as well. What beautiful words to a wounded spirit: Rejoice! Let us all lift up our hearts. Do not let our humility give way to anxiety or sadness. Jesus has cancelled the handwriting which was against us. To Lewis, it is a slap in God's face to not enjoy him, no matter where one is on their spiritual journey.

I remember when my friend Bobby had four felonies removed from his record. There was no real reason for him to have them taken off but for the fact that he wanted them gone. It was not affecting his career or relationships . . . just affecting the back of his mind. So, he started the legal process to have them expunged. It took some meetings, some cold hard cash, a pile of legal paperwork, and a lot of divine providence, but after jumping through all the legal hoops and paperwork, he was told they were removed.

He wanted to see it for himself, however, so he drove down to the county court house that maintained his records, paid the sixteen dollars it took for a print out, and waited for the results. After a few minutes, the clerk finally handed him a document that said "History of Arrest" at the top and went on to list all the offenses that were on his arrest record. However, in the section that would have any criminal offenses listed, there was nothing but white paper. It was blank. It was beautiful. He wanted to double check so he asked her to look again. He would have paid another sixteen dollars. After clicking around a bit, the lady behind the glass said, "Sir, we have no record that you were ever arrested."

There was nothing. Although he knew he had been arrested and was in and out of the justice system for years, and although he remembered the tight handcuffs, the officers that took him into custody, and the cellmates he spent time with, this printout said nothing had ever happened . . . it had been erased. That moment brought rejoicing to his spirit. He knew he had arrests in his past, but this ever important paper said that he did not. The handwriting had been canceled.

There's a line from a hymn that I try to remember that goes like this:

"Well may the accuser roar

2. Phil 4:4.

of sins that I have done.

I know them all and thousands more;

Jehovah knoweth none."[3]

I remember one of my favorite pastors speaking at a conference I attended in Jacksonville, Florida. He told a joke of a wealthy man wanting to buy a car in France but having trouble figuring out which car to purchase. He researched car after car, review after review, and ad after ad. He finally landed on the Rolls-Royce. This was because the Rolls-Royce was advertised as the car that would never break down. Since 1906 not one person could ever find one instance of a Rolls-Royce ever having any mechanical issues. The rich man was sold.

So surprised was he when he was cruising up and down the beautiful hills of Southern France and the car that never breaks down broke down. He was flabbergasted. He was furious. He immediately called his dealership to report that the luxury car he had purchased had broken down. The dealership said they would send the mechanics as soon as they were able. Incensed, the car owner hung up the phone and waited.

He didn't wait long, however. Within minutes of his phone call ending, several helicopters appeared overhead and a team of mechanics fast-roped down with their tool bags, immediately starting to tinker under his hood. It didn't take long until the Rolls-Royce was up and running and the mechanics were sky-hooked out of there.

Needless to say, the car owner was pleased with the prompt and reliable service that came with the car. So, he drove home and waited for the bill to come in the mail . . . he waited . . . and then he waited . . . and then he waited some more. Finally, as a person of means who was ready to get this bill behind him, he called up Rolls-Royce. He reminded them that a team of fast-roping mechanics had descended upon his broken-down car, fixed it, and were pulled out of there as quickly as they had arrived. He was pleased with their service and was ready for the bill. However, the operator on the other wasted no time in saying, "We're sorry, sir, but we have no record of anything ever having gone wrong with your car."

As cheesy as that joke is, it is wonderful to think about a record of impurities being completely gone. It is one thing for the prisoner to be released from prison—that should be celebrated—but to be released and also have one's record completely erased? Well, that is something divine indeed.

---

3. http://www.restorationchurchdc.com/wp-content/uploads/2013/04/His-Be-the-Victors-Name.pdf.

It is a beautiful thing to think that one day, we will be standing before our heart's desire, trembling, unworthy, the reel of all our past mistakes replaying in our head, only to hear him say, "We have no record that anything has ever gone wrong." That is an emotional thought indeed—an emotional thought that can be applied to one's logic and actually convince the inner spirit to celebrate, take a breath, and relax in this beautiful inevitability.

The handwriting against us has been canceled, so we are required to rejoice. What a welcomed commandment. What good is a relationship with God, the one and only relationship we were designed to be fulfilled by, if we sulk our way through the relationship, beating ourselves up because of our mistakes? What a poor excuse for a relationship. I would not imagine a relationship like that would be worth dying for, and I do not believe Christ did die for that sort of relationship. How much we cheapen our relationship with God by not enjoying the price that was paid to remove our mistakes. Lewis writes:

> I think we all sin by needlessly disobeying the apostolic injunction to "rejoice" as much as by anything else. Humility, after the first shock, is a cheerful virtue.[4]

For all of the fundamentalists out there who need a checklist of "This is a sin/This is not a sin," here's a reminder: "We all sin by needlessly disobeying the apostolic injunction to 'rejoice.'" If we're ever confused as to what is a mistake, what is a sin, what makes God angry, etc., Lewis is reminding us here that out of all the injunctions we should strive to follow in the Scriptures, the command to "rejoice" is as strong as any other commandment. How dare we not obey the command to rejoice in him.

One day I was shopping at one of my country's major department chains. While this particular department store does in fact guarantee my satisfaction, the experience itself is always a little stressful, especially on the weekends after payday. In the rare occasion that I find myself alone in this undesirable shopping endeavor, I escape into my headphones and pretend I am anywhere else but there. This particular day however, I was with my son and his little friend at the time, Derrick. They were both running around

---

4. Lewis, *Problem of Pain*, 63.

the aisles next to me, but as long as they were in earshot, I allowed them to roam. My boy, however, found a way to try my patience.

As if wrestling through the aisles with two small boys at this busy store was not tiresome enough, and as if the motorized cart people who park in the middle of the aisle while reading ingredients wasn't annoying enough, somewhere along the way my son had picked up a blue rubber duck that made a piercing squeaky sound when compressed. My boy sure enjoyed compressing that particular duck.

Squeak squeak, squeak squeak, I heard throughout our venture. *Squeak squeak, squeak squeak*. More cart people reading more ingredients. *Squeak squeak, squeak squeak*. More store associates parking their pallets in the middle of the bread aisle. *Squeak squeak, squeak squeak*. More people walking approximately 10 percent slower than I. *Squeak squeak, squeak squeak* . . . I finally had to intervene.

"Put the duck down buddy," I said as we shuffled through the frozen meat department. But a few minutes later . . . *squeak squeak, squeak squeak*.

"Mason buddy, make sure you put that duck down." I continued to fill my cart with enriched flour products and then . . . *squeak squeak, squeak squeak*.

"Mason," I demanded, "put down the duck!"

The duck went quiet for a bit. Eventually I went back to the task at hand and thought about the quickest way to escape the massive formations of shoppers checking-out. When I eventually began stacking my groceries on the conveyer belt, I heard the boys giggle, and then I heard the all-too-familiar sound of a rubber duck being squeezed between the sticky fingers of my seven-year-old . . . *squeak squeak, squeak squeak*.

"Mason, we're not getting the duck. Lay it down and help me get these groceries on here."

Derrick and Mason both began to help me offload the groceries on the belt and then back into the cart after I had paid. We made it to the car. I loaded up the groceries, loaded up the kids, and pulled out of the parking lot. I hooked a right onto 12th Ave. and approached the first stoplight, when, what sound befell my disbelieving ears? . . . *squeak squeak, squeak squeak*.

You have got to be kidding me, I thought. I clenched my jaw. *He took that duck!* I gathered myself and made sure not to blow up or embarrass my boy in front of his buddy.

"Mason," I said sternly. "Did you steal that duck?" He went silent. The word *steal* had not entered his mind until that point. The giggles that had previously accompanied the squeaks dissipated. I drove down the road in silence and tried to best figure out how to handle the thievery that had just taken place under my watch. I weighed my options.

One time, when I was a teenager, a little boy stole a disposable camera at the Family Dollar I was working for in Kingston, Oklahoma. The boy's dad requested that we call the police and that the police handcuff his small boy to scare the desire to steal again out of his son . . . *I could do that*, I thought. That was quite tempting.

He had a Ninja Turtle piggy bank at home. *We could go get that, have him bring it to the store, and make him pay for his new squawky mallard friend* . . . No. That would require me to go back into that store, and I just didn't feel up to punishing the boy and myself at the same time . . . *so what do I do?*

Then it hit me. I had just read something in Max Lucado's book, *Grace*, and I had been looking for the perfect time to implement it . . . and possibly win the Father of the Year award. So, I executed:

"Son, do you have that duck in your hands right now?"

Silence. He knew the answer, but the gravity of the situation was setting in.

"Mason, I need you to answer me. Do you have that duck in your hands right now?"

"Yes," he was able to murmur.

"And did Daddy pay for that duck?"

"No."

"So, when you take something from the store without paying for it, what is that called?"

Silence, and then he answered, "Stealing."

"Yes," I proclaimed, "stealing." But then was able to improvise beyond Max Lucadon's version. "You know Daddy is in prisons all the time, right?"

"Yes, Daddy."

"And do you know what one of the biggest crimes in prison is?"

He didn't say anything, but at this point Derrick had picked up what I was putting down.

"Stealing," Derrick contributed.

"That's right. Stealing. People who steal go to jail." I let that sink in for a second . . . then I continued, "And what did you do?"

"I stole," Mason answered.

"That's right. You stole that duck. So, what do you think your punishment should be?"

"Jail." His little precious voice was shaky at this point, and I almost broke character.

"That's right. People who steal go to jail. You stole that duck. So, your punishment should be to go to jail." Now, I know I am laying it on pretty thick, and this situation didn't necessarily call for a lesson of this deep emotional gravity, but I was wanting him to come to terms with what he deserved.

I let him sweat out. I let him envision life behind bars: the thin mattresses, the fights in the yard, the chain gangs, and the lockdowns. I finally let him up for air.

"Son," I continued, "do you know what grace is?"

"No." He whispered.

"Grace is not getting what we deserve," I preached. "You stole that duck, and you deserve to go to jail. However, I choose to give you grace. I am not going to punish you. I am going to pay for that duck next time I go in there, and not only are you not going to get punished for your crime, I choose to not even treat you as a criminal." Then I landed the celebratory plane, "In fact, I am going to forget this whole thing right here, right now. You're not in trouble! You're my son. I love you, and because I'm paying for your mistakes, you do not have to be treated like a criminal ever again."

Then I connected the dots for him, "And Buddy, that's exactly what God has done for us. We have all made mistakes and all deserve a grave punishment. We all deserve to live an eternity away from God. But because of what Jesus did on the cross, we can go to God for forgiveness and he will give us grace. That's what grace is Buddy!" Smile on my face, Father of the Year certainly in my future, I drove on, satisfied with the lesson I had just landed, and waited for the inevitable celebrations coming from the backseat. Perhaps a snow cone would solidify his father's grace and patience with him—my son would be certain to love me more and celebrate my kindness and forgiveness with his friend Derrick. If they could have lifted me up on their shoulders and march me down the street, they would have.

However, from the backseat: *silence.*

The silence coming from the two boys was not what I expected. Perplexed and a little let down, I continued.

"Buddy, not only does God forgive us of our mistakes, but he chooses to look at us and treat us as if we never made any mistakes at all. He gives us grace! And that's what I am giving you! Isn't that cool?"

Nothing. He pulled down his little ball cap and stared out the window. He had obviously missed the lesson. He had obviously missed the good news.

I drove down the street expecting a different result from my hard-taught lesson. I thought he would be ecstatic after learning the gravity of his crime and realizing the results were no punishment, no negative thoughts, just pure grace. I was expecting him to reach up and hug me by the neck and we would all go celebrate over a snow cone. I thought Derrick would automatically be in awe of my parenting skills and immediately come to the conclusion that I was a much better dad than his. My boy had been afforded grace! He had committed such a crime and I chose not to prosecute! But no. Just silence, his head hung low.

"Buddy, what's wrong?"

A pause.

"I deserve to go to jail."

That hurt me.

"Yes, buddy, but that's not the point. The point is I am not going to punish you. The point is I am choosing to give you grace and forget your mistakes."

Silence.

I was troubled. I thought it was a good opportunity for a lesson, but he totally missed the beauty of grace. There he was, focused on what he did wrong instead of the grace that was offered to him. Why was he not happy? Why was he not rejoicing? He stole something and I was not going to punish him. I was going to purchase it for him. Why the depression? . . . you see the point.

Wow . . . I do that every day with God. I make a mistake. I go to God for forgiveness. I say that I trust in the redemptive power of the cross. I tell others I'm forgiven. I tell others that they are forgiven. Yet, in my alone time, in the backseat of the car, I slump my head down in disappointment. *I deserve to go to jail.* Instead of looking up at the good Father who did everything in his power to make sure that I would not have to be punished for my mistakes, I sit there like a little boy in the backseat, hat pulled down in front of my face, feeling like a third-string Christian, sulking because of my sins, neglecting the joy that should be at the forefront of my heart because I've been deemed not guilty.

Knowing how badly I wanted my son to feel the weight removed in that moment, to feel joy fill up his heart because he was not going to be punished, and just enjoy me as his father, gave me pause to think about how I treat my relationship with God. I was the most expensive soul in history. He willingly chose to purchase me with his blood. Yet, I sulk. I miss out on one of the best benefits of knowing Christ. I miss out on enjoying the Father. I know the handwriting has been erased. What would it look like if I acted like it? I know full well what I deserve while simultaneously knowing full well that the charges were dropped. How much fuller could my life be if I relaxed in that? Christ Jesus literally gave his life to forgive me of my sins, and I have the nerve to walk around sulking, still focused on the wrong that I have committed. The cost of cancelling the handwriting against me was the greatest cost in all of history. While we can never fully pay God back for what he did, it seems that, at the very least, we can enjoy it. We can take up the apostolic command to rejoice . . . rejoice in him . . . rejoice in life . . . rejoice that one day, on this side of the pearly gates, when everything that we have ever done wrong is in the forefront of our minds, there will be a gate-keeper who will say, "I find no record of anything ever having gone wrong."

10

Noticing the Dirt

No man knows how bad he is till he has tried very hard to be good.

—C. S. LEWIS, *MERE CHRISTIANITY*[1]

L EWIS is a master at forcing people to dream bigger, to think larger and more expansively. One thing he did for me was take the negative view of my spiritual struggles and flip them into a positive. Lewis writes, "Only those who try to resist temptation know how strong it is. After all, you find out the strength of the German army by fighting against it, not by giving in."[2] Lewis would ask me, "Why are you so aware of the darkness inside of yourself? Why are you so aware of the sin that remains? Why is there such a large gulf between where you are and where you want to be?" The answer is because I am in the business of wanting to clean myself up. It is people like me, who generally want to do good and generally want to follow Christ, that are constantly reminded how depraved and dirty we really are. We know the strength of the German army because we have fought against it. We may have been completely steamrolled by the German army, but the attempt was made to stand our ground. We were in the resistance. When a Christian stumbles, he or she should be comforted by the fact that he or she can recognize a stumble in the first place. That's a healthy platform to fight back from next time.

1. Lewis, *Mere Christianity*, 142.
2. Lewis, *Mere Christianity*, 142.

We know our ability to fall into temptation because we want to stay out of it. "That is why bad people, in one sense, know very little about badness—they have lived a sheltered life by always giving in. We never find out the strength of the evil impulse inside us until we try to fight it."[3] It would be a scary place indeed to never fight against the rebel that lies within us. Bad people do not realize they are bad people, because they are not in the business of standing up against their badness. Those who generally delight in pleasing God will constantly be exposed to the darkness they carry around with them. This is some beautiful silver lining in the fight against our natural selves. In a world of endless hatred and a universe seemingly filled with chaos, we have found a way to focus on the good. That's got to mean something.

I think this is why Christ's teachings like The Sermon on the Mount[4] are so important. Jesus hits his listeners with a pretty tall order. His commands, at times, seem nearly impossible to keep. He commands us to always turn our cheek when attacked. He implores us not to store up treasures here in this life. He tells us that we cannot serve both God and money. And just in case he does not snag his listeners with "do not lust" and "do not hate," he commands us to "Be perfect,"[5] just like his Father in heaven is perfect. Christ commands perfection?

While it is important to strive to keep his commands, as the Christian's walk with Christ will be so much more substantial and fulfilling if one does, I believe these commands are not meant to be a checklist for God-pleasing spirituality. I believe they are meant to be a mirror that exposes our flaws. They are supposed to illustrate the perfection that we are unable to achieve on our own. They are supposed to expose our weakness. They are supposed to expose our need for a savior. That is the only usefulness of this temporary monkey on our backs called shame. That is the usefulness of realizing how depraved we really are. It points us to Christ . . . the only one who can do anything about it.

My grandma used to have a magnifying mirror in her bathroom while I was growing up. I remember flipping the mirror back and forth as a kid. One side was a normal mirror; the other would magnify ten times the normal reflection. The normal side would reveal a cute, freckle-faced, sun-kissed

3. Lewis, *Mere Christianity*, 142.
4. Matt 5–7.
5. Matt 5:48.

kid of eight or nine years old. The magnified side would reveal a greasy, dirty-faced boy who needed to rid his nose of a multitude of blackheads. It was not a pretty sight. I shudder to think what that reflection would show if I looked at it today. The reason those mirrors are not more popular, I imagine, is that they reveal too much. We're uncomfortable looking that deeply into our flaws. The gospel does just that. It reveals the deepest, perhaps previously unseen, flaws and reveals our need for a savior.

Paul writes, "Although I want to do good, evil is right there with me. For in my inner being I delight in God's law; but I see another law at work in me, waging war against the law of my mind and making me a prisoner of the law of sin at work within me."[6] He wants to do good, like any follower of Christ who delights in God's law. Yet the awareness of sinfulness is constantly there. Why? To be a constant reminder to submit to Christ, a constant realization that we need a savior, after all. "Who will rescue me from this body that is subject to death? Thanks be to God, who delivers me through Jesus Christ our Lord!"[7] Being able to see the deplorable in my life means I am still in the resistance. My surrender is not to the sin that would overtake me and remove my ability to detect it. My surrender is still to God, no matter how tough the opposing forces seem to be. A solid remedy for my low spiritual self-esteem, that Lewis and Paul both helped me understand, is to see the awareness of my sinful humanity as a positive, a sheer sign that God is nearer than I ever dare dream. After all, as Lewis reminds us, "It is when we notice the dirt that God is most present in us: it is the very sign of His presence."[8]

Our flaws can be a positive tool. Our flaws can be a routine reminder that we do not have any of this under control. We are incapable of rescuing ourselves, hence we need a Rescuer. If we can navigate the mental gymnastics, every time we fail can be cause to grow closer to the One who never does. The mere fact that we know we are flawed is a very healthy sign that we are near the presence of God. This remedy alone did wonders for my healing process, but the biggest blow to my condition came from Lewis showing me how extremely prideful I was being. I never thought low self-esteem could be connected with pride, but Lewis made the connection.

6. Rom 7:21–23.

7. Rom 7:24–25.

8. Lewis, *Letters of C. S. Lewis,* 470.

11

Forget Your Pride

"Forget your pride (what have you to be proud of?) and forget your anger (who has done you wrong?) and accept the mercy of these good kings."

—ASLAN, *THE HORSE AND HIS BOY*[1]

EWIS had the right to be as prideful as any of his contemporaries. He was by all accounts a genius. He was a very popular professor, having students often sitting on the floor of his lecture halls just to hear him speak, and he was a very successful published author. Answering mountains of fan mail took up a large portion of his free time. Lewis, whether he accepted it or not, was something of a celebrity in his time. But he was very cautious against being prideful. He recognized this temptation as being one of the great traps Screwtape had to offer.

One might not realize it, but low self-esteem, indeed low spiritual self-esteem, can actually be caused by a tremendous amount of pride. This certainly is not the case every time. Self-esteem problems are certainly caused by a variety of reasons, many of which are outside of our control. But some people can feel low and never realize it is because of a substantial amount of narcissism and unhealthy pride that is really at the root. And this is good news. This is good news because if we realize it, we can fix it.

Lewis writes in *Mere Christianity*, "Do not imagine if you meet a really humble man he will be what most people call 'humble' nowadays . . . Probably all you will think about is that he seemed a cheerful, intelligent chap

---

1. Lewis, *Horse and His Boy,* 216.

who took a real interest in what you said to him."[2] An actual humble man will not be noticed as a humble man. He will just be noticed as a delightful fellow, more interested in the other people in the room than himself, focusing on their positives, not his own positives or negatives. Those with low spiritual self-esteem go about thinking bad about themselves, thinking how they do not measure up, thinking about how much other people have going for them and how little they do not, thinking about . . . well, thinking about themselves. Although it does not take the form of pride that most would recognize, it is a completely damaging and spiritually fatal form of pride. It seems humble. It seems meek, but all this inward focus is pride to the highest degree. It is still a form of, what Lewis would call, spiritual cancer.[3] Timothy Keller reflects on this:

> C. S. Lewis in *Mere Christianity*, makes a brilliant observation about gospel-humility at the very end of his chapter on pride. If we were to meet a truly humble person, Lewis says, we would never come away from meeting them thinking they were humble. They would not be always telling us they were a nobody (because a person who keeps saying they are a nobody is actually a self-obsessed person). The thing we would remember from meeting a truly gospel-humble person is how much they seemed to be totally interested in us. Because the essence of gospel-humility is not thinking more of myself or thinking less of myself, it is thinking of myself less.[4]

Keller, referencing Lewis, says, "a person who keeps saying they are a nobody is actually a self-obsessed person." Had I been an extremely self-obsessed person this whole time? By having negative thoughts about myself, was I actually participating in the ultimate form of narcissistic pride?

Lewis writes, "If you think you are not conceited, it means you are very conceited indeed."[5] Pride is like one of those pendulum balls people put on their desk. Whether the balls are swinging in one direction or the other, they are still swinging in an equal but opposite direction. Sometimes, if the very reason we feel bad about ourselves is swung in the complete opposite direction, it brings about huge amounts of pride. This is also the case if the same logic that brings about the negative feelings is applied to the positive feelings.

---

2. Lewis, *Mere Christianity*, 128.

3. Lewis, *Mere Christianity*, 125.

4. Keller, *The Freedom of Self Forgetfulness*, 32.

5. Lewis, *Mere Christianity*, 128.

Let's pretend that I pulled myself out of my low spiritual self-esteem on my own: one moment, in my mind, I am third-string Christian, down on myself because of my mistakes, not serving God to my full capacity because I am dirty. So, I pull myself out. I make myself extremely moral; I go two weeks without adding any mistakes to the morality scoreboard, and my church attendance goes up 50 percent. What are the logical results? What is the other side of the pendulum regarding feeling bad about my failures? It is feeling prideful about my perfection. I am not making mistakes. I am staying away from my known pitfalls; hence I am feeling good about myself . . . hence it is about me and what I have done . . . hence God owes me his favor . . . hence God owes me redemption. It is all about me. I have removed the dragon skin. There was no need for the claws of Aslan.

This is a spiritually fatal thought indeed and is pride to the highest degree. It's just pride in the opposite direction. For those like me, our pride has the tendency to accumulate on the other end of the spectrum than most would recognize, the negative end—but make no mistake, it is pride pure and simple. It is narcissism. My low spiritual self-esteem, generated by my failures and shortcomings, is just as cancerous as pride because we are moral. It is Pharisaical. It just takes a less recognizable form. The ultimate goal is to remove myself from the equation all together. Pride, whether in the form of the positive or in the form of the negative, has no place in the life of a follower of Christ.

Lewis writes, "Unchastity, anger, greed, drunkenness, and all that, are mere flea bites in comparison: it was through Pride that the devil became the devil: Pride leads to every other vice: it is the complete anti-God state of mind."[6] One of the most spiritually healthy remedies Lewis taught me to take was to remove pride from my walk with Christ altogether; to simply stop thinking about myself and to start focusing on others, and on my heart's desire. Once accomplished, and it must be accomplished daily, it was huge in slaying my low spiritual self-esteem.

Those who are prideful never have any fun. Whether the pride is directed outwards causing one to boast, or the pride is directed inward causing one to sulk, the disease of pridefulness causes one to stay in defense mode, taking oneself far too seriously, sucking the marrow out of life, and robbing one of the joys that God intended.

6. Lewis, *Mere Christianity*, 122.

Lewis is a great example of someone that, by all accounts, had the right to be uptight, prideful, and serious. His accomplishments would have tempted anyone to think that he was one step ahead of the common man, that his time was of more importance than the fans writing him letters. Yet that wasn't the case. He took the time to enjoy life, to hang out with his best friends, to return each and every letter he ever received. (Although sometimes it was via his brother Warnie's typewriter that these letters were returned. Lewis trusted his brother's ability and wit enough to return a letter on his behalf.)

He writes to a class of fifth graders in Maryland, "I'm tall, fat, rather bald, red-faced, double-chinned, black-haired, have a deep voice, and wear glasses for reading."[7] Here was a man comfortable in his own skin and ready to poke fun at himself. People who are able to poke fun at themselves have achieved a level of comfort and acceptance that I have always envied. People like this have set aside their pride and are much more apt to take on life with joy, optimism, and a lot of laughs along the way.

Lewis writes, "For pride is spiritual cancer: it eats up the very possibility of love, or contentment, or even common sense."[8] To win one's battle over low spiritual self-esteem, and in turn learn to laugh, to enjoy life, and enjoy God, the disease of pride has to be defeated. We have to let go of any notion that our spiritual successes and failures have anything to do with us or our abilities. It is all dependent on our simple surrender, our letting Aslan remove the skin, our learning to love the person in the mirror, not because the person is good, but because God is good, and he loves that person in the mirror, scars and all.

John Maxwell says that the final step towards stripping off one's pride comes when one is able to laugh at themselves. I like that. I imagine the first step to stripping off the pride and achieving real general humility looks different for everyone.

Lewis's first step to acquire humility is to realize that one is prideful. That is the first step and certainly one that many find the hardest. A second practical step that Lewis helped me learn was to be more proactively concerned with other people in the room than myself. I had to stop seeing people as someone taking up my talking time and see them as someone I could learn from. In meetings, I proactively bit my tongue. Instead of waiting for my time to speak and enlighten everyone in the room, I tried to go whole meetings without any sort of input. Yes, I wasn't seen as a strong leader with all the answers, but in my mind, I was more concerned with God removing

---

7. Lewis, *Letters to Children*, 45.

8. Lewis, *Mere Christianity*, 125.

the dragon skin of pride. When people in the community center that I was a part of would share their stories and the trouble they were experiencing, I learned to force myself to give them 100 percent of my attention, without thinking of my calendar or events for that day. When a prisoner who was not on my agenda for that day wanted a bit of my attention, I learned to stop in my tracks and make them my new agenda, although sometimes I still fail at this. If our schedules are so tight that we do not have time for everyday people who need an ear, we think we are far more important than we really are. I think John the Baptist said something about that . . . making ourselves less so that Christ can become more.

So, pride must be rooted out of our lives, even if pride takes a different form than what we normally think that pride takes. If we are prideful and we know it, we must do whatever is necessary to remove it from our personality. But we must never let it get us down too much. The mere fact that we recognize the pride in our lives is a positive development in our walk with Christ. Lewis writes to the British actress Sonia Graham, "Pride is a perpetual nagging temptation. Keep on knocking it on the head, but don't be too worried about it. As long as one knows one is proud, one is safe from the worst form of pride."[9] As long as we recognize the pride in our lives, both negative and positive, we are in much better shape than the person who is prideful but does not realize it. Those are to be pitied and prayed for more than anyone. May we never get there. May we take heart that we realize the moments when we are being prideful and narcissistic. May we keep knocking it on the head, and may we keep praising God that he died for people who will be knocking their sins of choice on the head from now till we meet him face to face.

One of the most helpful steps a third-string Christian who struggles with low spiritual self-esteem can take towards growing away from this sad state of being is realizing it is a sinfully prideful place to be. Not only is the Christian free from this nagging disease, he is encouraged to do so on the basis that true followers of Christ must strip away all forms of sinful pride, even the ones that take on different forms. What a beautiful command. The Christian is free to stop sulking. Christians are free to stop feeling like they are a failure because of their mistakes. Indeed, we are commanded not to. Christians are free to stop assuming God's plans are less for them because of their perpetual mistakes. Christians are free . . .

9. Lewis, *Letters of C. S. Lewis,* 539.

Preventative maintenance is a term I used to despise. In the Marines it normally meant cleaning something we had already cleaned three times that week and was impossible to clean anymore. When I got my Humvee license it meant going to motor transport once a week to check, change, and clean a vehicle that had not been driven since the last time we had checked, changed, and cleaned every square inch of it. Preventative maintenance was mundane, and at times seemed useless, but it was necessary. We were constantly performing maintenance on our gear during the boring times, so that we would not have to perform maintenance during the exciting times. Checking the engine coolant levels of a Humvee on base is much more pleasant, albeit boring, than trying to figure out why your vehicle is overheating in the middle of an ambush off base.

In the medical realm, preventative maintenance can be anything that will prevent someone from going back into the physical condition that they were just cured from. If one had to work really hard to get their blood pressure down, it would be helpful to know what kinds of foods and exercise they could add to their lives to keep it that way.

Once someone like me gets on top of their low spiritual self-esteem issues, it is important to add some preventative maintenance to their routine. Our natural slide is towards apathy. Our humanity is always knocking on the door, wanting back in. If we are not proactive, we will drift back towards the same slope that kept us down in the first place. In the next section, I'll discuss some (certainly not all) of the preventative maintenance steps that have assisted me with the ongoing struggle not to fall back into a sense of low spiritual self-esteem.

PART 4

Essays on Preventative Maintenance

12

Past Watchful Dragons

Balaam's ass, you remember, preached a very effective sermon in the midst of his 'hee-haws.'

—C. S. Lewis's final interview[1]

EARLIER I wrote about evil and how it's not a proactive thing. It does not take up space. It's what's left when goodness is drained out, much like a pile of gunk and leaves at the bottom of an emptied pool. Evil is not a proactive force but more of reactionary force. If we ever feel like an evil person or we are prone to do evil acts, the problem is not that we have too much evil stored up inside of us. The problem is that there is a lack of goodness inside of us. We are not proactively filling ourselves with goodness, so evil takes root. So, the best way to chase all traces of evil out of our systems (although we will never remove it all this side of eternity) is to inject goodness where evil is lurking.

One of the best ways, as far as I can tell, is to take our Christian faith on the offense and not on the defense (as I will explain we are prone to doing). Most of our Christian walk is defensive in nature. Eventually we need to let the defense take a rest and put the offense on the field. We need to move our faith forward. We needed to focus on the mission.

C. S. Lewis had a mission. He wanted to take theology and what it means to be a Christian and explain it in a way that the common man could understand . . . even children for that matter. He wanted to take theological

---

1. Wirt, "I Was Decided On," 1.

topics that are normally only accessible to the learned spiritual elites and put them on the bottom shelf for everyone to enjoy, and he was a master of doing so. It was one of his life's missions. He writes that, "The best, perhaps the only, service I can do for my unbelieving neighbors is to explain and defend the belief that has been common to nearly all Christians at all times."[2] This may not seem like a revolutionary idea today; after all, our Christian bookstores are full of short, easy to access books on what God may be like. But in Lewis's day, and especially given Lewis's profession, he was bucking the system in order to accomplish this mission. He was an academic. These popular books were below him, and certainly writing children's books was beneath the expectations of any Oxford Don. Lewis, however, did not care. He had a gift and he was going to use it to further the kingdom.

This was one reason why he wrote the Narnia books. Not at first, but he began to realize that he could smuggle a message into them. He realized children should have an opportunity to understand the Christian story outside the control of the Sunday school teachers that kept a tight monopoly on God knowledge. Lewis was not supposed to be meddling in teaching children theology. He was not a trained theologian. Yet, he wanted to slip Christ past those who stood in the way. Concerning his Narnia books and why he decided to smuggle in a Christian message, Lewis writes:

> Why did one find it so hard to feel as one was told one ought to feel about God or about the sufferings of Christ? I thought the chief reason was that one was told one ought to. An obligation to feel can freeze feelings . . . But supposing that by casting all these things into an imaginary world, stripping them of their stained-glass and Sunday school associations, one could make them for the first time appear in their real potency? Could one not thus steal past those watchful dragons? I thought one could.[3]

Lewis used his gifts and talents to sneak the message of Christianity past the "watchful dragons" that kept it in a chokehold. It certainly was not beneficial to his career.

Although Lewis is widely admired in Christian circles today, his reputation and his career suffered greatly because of his refusal to stop writing popular books and children's novels. He took heat from the Christian community on one end and the academic on the other. Yet he could not help it. His faith put him on the offense. He could have made a career as quiet but successful academic, sitting in the comfortable inner circles of Oxford, keeping his faith sidelined. But he chose to risk it all. He found his place in

2. Lewis, *Mere Christianity*, 6.
3. Lewis, *Of Other Worlds*, 34.

the kingdom, he found his gifts and talents, and he ran the ball forward. He was not content with a simple, quiet, inward-focused faith. He was not so much concerned with rooting out the evil inside him as he was concerned with adding goodness inside him, pushing forward his life's mission.

Many Christians live in this defensive version of Christianity, laying back, trying to not get injured. Their faith is mostly inwardly focused and is typically defined by their participation in a church that suits their needs. This version of Christianity is dumbed down to "do not sin here, do not sin there." There is plenty of inwardly focused discipleship, but not outwardly focused engagement. There is plenty of training for the battlefield, but never a foot stepped into enemy territory. It's like a well-skilled quarterback sitting on the sidelines because he is avoiding being hit. No matter how well-practiced and talented he is, what good is he if he doesn't engage and move the ball forward?

It is so easy to turn Christianity into what one does not do. I lived this view of Christianity for a long time. For the longest time, I was not proactively engaging my culture in a positive way because I was constantly on the sidelines, licking my wounds, focusing on what I had done wrong or what I would need to clean up. I was too busy servicing my wounds to ever think about servicing the wounds of another. I now believe that God is impressed very little by my ability not to sin. He is not impressed by the number of classes I've attended or books that I have read if all the while I sit on the sidelines, disengaged from the world around me that he has called me to reach. The more I read the Bible, the more I read Lewis and great heroes of the faith like Dietrich Bonhoeffer, Martin Luther, William Wilberforce, and MLK, the more I became convinced that Christianity was so much bigger than simply guarding against doing wrong. A larger, more beautiful, more robust image of God took shape in my mind. No matter our skill level, God did not send us into the game to sit on the sidelines.

I grew up on a lake where guided fishing trips were a large industry. It is not uncommon to drive down any given lake road and see guides in the driveways and open garages changing out the line in the reels, setting their rigs, organizing their tackle and cleaning their boats. If that was all that they did, if the guides never actually put clients in the boats and boats in the water, not only would they never make any money, they would be pitied and called fools. Certainly, their job is to do more than just prepare for fishing.

Certainly, the Christian's job is to do more than prepare to engage a world in need. Certainly, our job is to engage it.

Of course, all of this is not to say that Christians do not take the time to look inwardly. After all Jesus did tell us to clean the inside of our cup so that the outside might be clean too,[4] but for what purpose? Why do we take the time to clean ourselves up, as far as it depends on us? In one of his only surviving BBC Broadcasts given during World War II, Lewis made an argument addressing the complaint against Christianity being a selfish religion. He mentioned how the unbelievers of his day called Christianity self-centered and inward-focused. They even called it morbid, the way that Christians are always bothering about the inside of their soul instead of bothering about the rest of humanity. There is a world out there that needs fixing, but all the pious Christians do is spend time in their pews learning how to fix themselves. I partly agree with that complaint. It is very easy for a Christian to make their whole walk with Christ about them, instead of about others.

But Lewis suggested looking at the example of an NCO (non-commissioned officer) telling his soldier to clean his dirty rifle during his downtime in battle. Imagine the soldier replying with, "But sergeant, isn't it very selfish, even morbid, to be always bothering about the inside of your own rifle instead of thinking of the United Nations?" The NCO's response is not necessary. We can imagine what he would say, and we see the point. The soldier will not be good to the larger cause if they have an ineffective weapon.[5]

Following Christ does in fact demand that we take the time to clean the inside of our cup, or in Lewis's example, that we take the time to clean our rifles. But why? I love Lewis's analogy because when I, like Lewis, find myself in a literal combat situation, the importance of a clean rifle is crucial to combat effectiveness. It would be a horrid feeling to find myself in a firefight and pull the trigger, only to hear a "click" coming from my rifle, when I should have heard a "bang." At this point, I would immediately be out of the fight—a useless Marine holding a useless weapon. One should take the time to clean one's rifle but cleaning one's rifle for the sake of cleaning the rifle is a ridiculous thought indeed. The rifle serves an active purpose. All the clean rifles in all the armories in the world are meaningless unless someone takes them from the armory and puts them to use. If my Christianity is dwindled down to cleaning myself up but not actively engaging the world I was called to impact, my Christianity is useless. It is a clean weapon that never gets used. It's a well-trained quarterback who never gets to play.

4. Matt 23:26.
5. Apologetics315, "C. S. Lewis."

Dietrich Bonhoeffer certainly set an example of what offensive Christianity looks like. Shortly before he was hanged for his role in a plot to assassinate Hitler, using "chastity" as a mere example, he penned this line from his jail cell in Tegel prison: "The essence of chastity is not the suppression of lust, but the total orientation of one's life towards a goal. Without such a goal, chastity is bound to become ridiculous. Chastity is the sine qua non of lucidity and concentration."[6] Chastity for the sake of chastity is ridiculous. Not being prideful for the sake of not being prideful is ridiculous. Discipleship for the sake of discipleship is ridiculous. However, discipleship for the sake of becoming the best ambassador of Christ you can become makes much more sense. For Bonhoeffer, following Christ was less about inactively trying to avoid sin for the mere sake of doing so, but proactively living courageously for Christ. Avoiding sin when he was able was merely part of his training regimen.

Leaning about Lewis's proclivity towards service, learning how much he gave of his time and money, and learning about his desire to smuggle the message of Christ past the watchful dragons that stood between him and his children readers, despite the stunting it caused his career, challenged me, but excited me nonetheless. Once again, my healing journey kept returning to taking my focus off me and placing it firmly on Christ, my heart's desire, and others. I had to turn my focus more towards the kingdom and less towards me. For Lewis this meant taking the difficult-to-reach aspects of Christianity and putting them on the bottom shelf for everyone to enjoy. For Bonhoeffer it meant keeping the integrity of the church, during a time when Nazi Germany was turning Christianity upside down. For Martin Luther it meant taking the Scriptures out of the hands of the religious elites and putting them in the hands of the everyday person. For William Wilberforce it meant helping to abolish an industry of slave trade that did not mesh with the message of Christ. For MLK it meant fighting for equality for all who are made in the image of God, using Scripture as his fuel. For me, it currently means reaching out and serving the marginalized in our society such as prisoners forgotten behind bars and teenagers in our inner cities growing up below the poverty line. I had been doing this before, but my confidence and my purpose perked up. I was less concerned with my shortcomings and more concerned with my mission. It was full steam ahead. God was not waiting for me to reach a state of spiritual perfection before he used me to

6. Bonhoeffer, *Papers and* Letters, 369.

make an impact in this world. If that were the way God operated, he would have very few people to use to bring about his purposes . . . in fact, in all of history, he would have only had the One.

I know this may sound intimidating to someone who is more used to playing defense than offense with their Christian faith. We have all been there for sure. But the Christian should take heart. Going on the offensive does not have to translate into jumping into the state prison system like me or trying to take out Hitler like Bonhoeffer. Offensive Christianity could be something as simple as proactively raising godly children, making it a point to pray for the sick in the hospital, or picking up a student for church on Sundays who otherwise would never attend. None of these are small. They are all huge versions of offensive Christianity.

Christians should ask themselves, why all the church? Why all the training? Why all the fill-in-the-blanks in our worship folders, and the inspirational quotes online? So we can continue the inward focus? Or so we can go on the offense with our Christian faith and engage a world that needs some serious healing? Big steps. Small steps. It should not matter. In the "Parable of the Talents,"[7] the only man to let down the master was the man who played defense with his talent and didn't put it to use. Oswald Chambers writes:

> Have you ever realized that you can give things to God that are of value to Him? Or are you just sitting around daydreaming about the greatness of his redemption, while neglecting all the things you could be doing for him? I'm not referring to work which could be regarded as divine and miraculous, but ordinary, simple human things—things which would be evidence to God that you are totally surrendered to Him.[8]

Christians should always be looking for a way to take their eyes off themselves and live out an offensive form of their Christian faith, big or small. Indeed, God accepts both.

A preventative maintenance step I try to keep in place to combat my spiritual condition is staying proactive in my faith, focusing on what I can give to God rather than where I am failing, and not focusing on where I am coming up short but on the good things I can bring to God, whether I am feeling spiritual healthy at all. This will long outlast my sinful nature. Our smallest act of goodness will outlast all the evil in the world by an eternity. The interesting thing is those pesky recurring sins that used to take up a lot of spiritual capacity have almost taken care of themselves once my view of God expands and I begin to focus on the offense.

---

7. Matt 25:14–30.

8. Chambers, *My Utmost*, 75.

13

A Germ of Desire

The whole thickening treatment consists in learning to want God for His own sake.

—C. S. LEWIS, *THE GREAT DIVORCE*[1]

IT's always been easy for me to fall into the ever-familiar trap of wanting the things of God more than I wanted God. Of course, I would never admit this—most self-respecting Christians would not, yet still, it happens. It would be very easy in our culture to wake up one day and realize that we have been desiring the things of God more than we desire God. The idea of serving the Almighty God certainly has its perks. All Christians want the forgiveness that comes from knowing God. Everyone wants to feel whole, to feel redeemed, and certainly everyone would want to live in some concept of heaven one day. Then add in all the bonuses of our Christian culture which can be desirable to many in and of themselves . . . but to desire God for the mere sake of desiring God . . . that is not something that always comes easy.

Let's face it, our churches do offer some very appealing social structures. They fill a relational void than many people struggle to find elsewhere, and that in itself is a good thing. We're surrounded by Christian versions of secular things. There are Christian dating sites in competition with secular dating sites. There are Christian movie streaming sites to give the faithful a clean alternative to mainstream streaming sites. There are Christian

1. Lewis, *Great Divorce*, 99.

bookstores that sell Christian versions of secular goods, even selling Christian-themed candy! (I remember one time picking up a pack of spearmint "Test-a-Mints" that promised to give me heavenly breath.) I am not anti any of these things, in fact I feel some of them do a great deal of good. But I am making a point to say it would be very easy for a Christian to get lost in the sea that is Christian culture and not realize that their true heart's desire was never for God . . . but only for the lifestyle that the Christian culture provides.

It is important that all Christians check their motives thoroughly and often, especially Christians like me in professional ministry or anyone whose wholesome public persona is tied to their professional success. If I did not attend church, chances are I would not have a job. If I was blatantly rude in public or online, chances are someone would complain to my boss that I was being unbecoming for a pastor. If I had no prayer life or did not give thanks to God before I ate at a church Wednesday night dinner, people would notice. I have to face the fact that I get paid to try and be a pretty good Christian. People in professional ministry or public life have an extreme handicap when it comes to desiring God simply for his own sake. C. S. Lewis taught me to check myself, thoroughly and often.

In *The Great Divorce* we meet a ghost named Pam who takes the bus from hell to visit heaven with one goal in mind. She does not want to see the glorious landscapes. She does not want to visit the friendly spirits that welcome the passengers, and she certainly does not care to see or meet God. She wants her son Michael.[2] However, Michael, who is a solid spirit at this point, is deep in the mountains worshiping God and is unable to come see his ghostly mother. Pam will have none of this though. She is *going* to see her son. The problem is, she is a ghost. She has trouble walking on grass. It looks like the soft grass we are all accustomed to, yet it slices through her feet with every step. There is no way she is going to tip-toe her way, further up and further in, to the vast, heavenly landscape on the horizon. She wants and needs to "thicken up"[3] and become a solid spirit like her hosts if she ever has any hopes of traveling into the mountains to get to her son Michael.

As a father, I can empathize with Pam. I am very much tempted to live more for my son that I am for God, and I often do. Not on purpose. But when I take the time to stop and check my motives, my bank account,

2. Lewis, *Great Divorce*, 97–104.

3. Lewis, *Great Divorce*, 98–99.

and how I spend my time, it normally paints the picture of a person who serves his son as often or more than God. I am certain I would want to do the same thing as Pam. I would want to thicken up . . . and go get my boy. However, the heavenly sprits that are hosting her inform her that this will not be possible. She will have to become one of them if she is ever to see her son. Yet, to become one of them she will have to take the first step. She cannot simply thicken up to a solid body without that crucial first step. She has to surrender her life to God, or at least take the first small step towards doing so. The Spirit encourages her, "I'm afraid the first step is a hard one, but after that you'll go on like a house on fire. You will become solid enough for Michael to perceive you when you learn to want Someone Else besides Michael."[4] She has to learn to desire God alongside her desire for Michael.

Notice two things that the Spirit says that should be great news for Pam and for someone like me: we can *learn* to desire God. It does not have to be a full-fledged, deep desire that may sound intimidating at first, especially when we're so far away from the mountains. It can be a miniscule amount of desire for God. In fact, the Spirit goes on to say, "It's only the little germ of a desire for God that we need to start the process."[5] People like Pam and I just need to muster a small amount of desire, and let the learning begin. After that, we can go on "like a house on fire."

The other point the Spirit is trying to make to Pam, which continues to be good news, is that she must learn to want someone else *besides* Michael. The Spirit does not even demand that Pam desire God *more* than Michael . . . simply alongside him. When I reach a point that the things of God are more enticing than God himself, I can take comfort that I am not expected quite yet to want those things less than God. I can learn to want God alongside the natural instinct to desire something else. The Spirit tells Pam that desiring God more than Michael will come later. She just needs to start with a small desire for her Creator, then everything will come about in time. Unfortunately, we never know if Pam ever takes this step forward. She is only using God as a means to Michael, never wanting God for his own sake.

The story of Pam in *The Great Divorce* is reminiscent of the elder brother in the story of The Prodigal Son.[6] He will not share his Father's happiness because he cannot believe that, after all his work for his Father, the Father

---

4. Lewis, *Great Divorce*, 98.

5. Lewis, *Great Divorce*, 98.

6. Luke 15:11–32.

would celebrate the younger brother, not him. He is working for the Father but doing so with an inward focus and career advancement at heart. He very well could have been in professional ministry. The older son, who is equally invited to the celebration as much as the younger son, desires the things of the Father more than he desires his Father. We are never told whether or not he makes it to the celebration.

It is important for us to begin to regularly ask ourselves questions like, "Am I using God as a means to a successful career like the older son?"; "Am I using God as a means of raising a moral child like Pam?"; "Am I using God because the lifestyle that cultural Christianity brings is more my thing than the things of the world?"; "Am I using God as a means of anything other than simply desiring God?" I have learned to ask myself these questions often, and if I am honest with myself, I can identify several times when the answer to those questions is, "Most likely, yes. I am more interested in the things of God rather than simply God." Yet, there is no reason to be downcast. This is the importance of asking ourselves those questions. We can make adjustments. I can pray for help. I can take the Spirit's advice from *The Great Divorce* and learn to desire the Father more than I desire the things of the Father. All I need is germ of a desire. Lewis writes to a little fan of his Narnia series:

> God knows quite well how hard we find it to love Him more than anyone or anything else, and He won't be angry with us as long as we're trying. And He will help us.[7]

Perhaps we all have a small child inside of us who can benefit from the words of Lewis. Let us see if we can conjure up just a germ of desire to desire God simply for the sake of desiring him. Ask him for help if we need. Let the learning begin, and eventually, burn for him like a house on fire. Checking our motives thoroughly and often is a great preventative maintenance step on our journey of going further up and further in towards our Creator.

---

7. Lewis, *Letters to Children*, 52.

14

Friendship is Unnecessary

My happiest hours are spent with three or four old friends in old clothes tramping together and putting up in small pubs—or else sitting up till the small hours in someone's college rooms talking nonsense, poetry, theology, metaphysics over beer, tea, and pipes. There's no sound I like better than adult male laughter.

—C. S. LEWIS, WRITTEN TO HIS AMERICAN PUBLISHER ON THE DUST JACKET OF *PERELANDRA* [1]

FRIENDSHIPS meant the world to Lewis. For the vast majority of his life, all of his closest relationships were made up of friends who he wrote to, served alongside in the military, taught with, and grew old with. He was never without a close friend to confide in, laugh with, drink with, or talk theology or poetry. It was these close relationships that led him to become a theist in the first place. It was his friendship with J. R. R. Tolkien that led to Lewis accepting Christ. This relationship was also a motivating factor that led Tolkien to write, and eventually finish, *The Lord of the Rings* after he was done with *The Hobbit*.

For Lewis, a necessary ingredient for following Christ was to achieve and maintain deep and meaningful friendships that sharpened him, challenged him, and brought joy to his heart. These relationships were most likely the sustaining force behind Lewis's ability to remain a bachelor for the majority of his life. Lewis saw love between friends as something that took very little effort. It was not beneficial for either member besides that which

---

1. Lewis, *Letters to Arthur,* 26–27.

comes from the simple benefits of love. It has no duties attached to it besides those which are attached to love. It is almost completely free from jealousy and the qualification of the need to be needed. A love like this, he assumed, was the sort of love enjoyed by the angels.[2]

These relationships were essential for his spiritual well-being, as they are essential to ours as well. One of the most crucial character traits I picked up from studying C. S. Lewis for three years was that of desiring and maintaining deep and challenging friendships . . . the right kind of friendships for the right reasons. As I will go on to explain, this is not always easy, but it is a crucial preventative maintenance tool to have in our spiritual tool belts.

The Eagle and Child

I walked into the Eagle and Child Pub in downtown Oxford with great anticipation. It was a lot smaller than I expected and looked like just about every other neighborhood pub I had been to on that particular trip to England. My fellow Lewis students and I stood in a dimly lit line, backed up to patrons already enjoying their order at their tables, waiting to place our order before finding a table. When we eventually made it to the cashier, we all ordered some freshly cut chips and a drink. The pub smelled old. It smelled historic. I was happy that the owners tried to maintain the original feel of the place and did not let it become the touristy, money-making pit that it could be. It appeared as if great care had been put into keeping this pub looking and feeling very much like it looked in the 1930s.

However, on the wall hung small tributes to the famous patrons that used to sneak away from work mid-day, every Tuesday, to have a quick beer or tea and great conversation about literature, poetry, or religion. There were pictures of Lewis, J. R. R. Tolkien, Owen Barfield, Hugo Dyson, Charles Wilson, and more. This group of friends would go down in history as one of the most infamous literary groups ever. They called themselves the Inklings. If one took the time to look at all the pictures and articles on the wall, one could read all about the famous Inklings group that met here throughout the 1930s and 40s. It was the conversations that took place in this pub that produced classics like *The Lord of the Rings, Out of the Silent Planet*, and of course, *The Chronicles of Narnia*. To be a fly on the wall of that place, to witness some of the great literary classics of all time being discussed, critiqued, given up on, and encouraged would be a thing of literary dreams.

I sat down next to a pastor friend from New Zealand, ministers from Texas and California, a head pastor from the Netherlands, and a children's

2. Lewis, *Four Loves*, 111.

minister from Hong Kong. At first, we sipped our drinks quietly and dipped our chips into brown sauce. We were all having a moment. We had all traveled great distances to study Lewis at Oxford and Cambridge, and this pub was certainly one of the highlights of our Lewis journey.

The atmosphere around us remained politely quiet for quite some time. It was not uncomfortable. It was actually very pleasant. The loud conversations and laughter coming from all the other tables surrounding us seemed muffled and distant. If any place was appropriate to shrug off a busy day of study and lectures about Lewis, and enjoy the tastes and sounds of an English pub, the Eagle and Child was the place to do so . . . here, where so many great and important relationships were developed, solidified, and cherished and so many great works of literature and theology were discussed and created . . . far away from work . . . far away from domestic responsibilities . . . just a fellowship of friends who happened to be Christian and shared a love for God, literature, and poetry.

The atmosphere remained reverent until one of my new friends returned from the toilet with a picture on his phone of the porcelain urinal that extended all the way to the floor. He showed the group and asked in an unmistakable New Zealand accent, "Hey mates, do you think this was where Lewis and Tolkien used to pee?!" We all laughed. Then we began to discuss if they would have replaced the urinal in the last 70 years or so, or if they even had porcelain urinals back then. It was a great experience, but what made it best was that I was surrounded by friends who shared common interests with me and who could make me laugh.

Laughter is crucial in any relationship. I don't see a point in having a relationship without large amounts of laughter. I feel all relationships are striving to get to a vulnerable place where they can finally relax and laugh loud, hard, and often. That's where the sweet spot of the relationship lies. That's where we are all yearning to be in all of our relationships.

We stayed there for about an hour or so, laughing, talking about our favorite books, talking about the lectures, enjoying each other, and enjoying Lewis and Tolkien. The Eagle and Child is a must for any Lewis fan that finds herself or himself in Oxford.

~

Some portrayals of Lewis, both in literature and in film, leave the audience convinced that he was a stuffy, Oxford Don, retreating into his room to read and write, only coming out to teach, scorn, and grade his students. This was most definitely not the case. Lewis was extremely social. He saw great value in his friendships and cherished them very deeply. Most biographers note how Lewis's most deep and meaningful friendships developed only after his conversion to Christianity. However, it was after he found the joy of being known and accepted by a living God that Lewis was able to shed the pessimism that was attached to his atheism and develop his boyish, joyful traits that enabled him to engage in such sustaining friendships. Lewis's bliss and euphoria towards life is one of the traits I am most envious of. I try to apply it to my life as often as I can. Laughing at this passing world is a great way to stick it towards the enemy. But one cannot laugh alone. One must have the vulnerable relationships that allow this sort of joy. Lewis is a great model of someone who maintained many of these relationships.

There was one friend, however, who Lewis maintained on both sides of his conversion. Lewis was able to keep a relationship for the majority of his life with his friend Arthur Greeves, who remained back in Ireland as Lewis moved around England. We, as future Lewis fans, were fortunate enough that these two wrote many letters back and forth to each other for nearly fifty years, and we're even more fortunate that these letters were maintained and eventually published. C. S. Lewis's friendship with Arthur Greeves looks awfully close to what we would call an accountability relationship today. They opened up to each other about anything and everything, sharing details about their life that we would reserve only for the closest of friends. They would write back and forth about how much Lewis hated England, initially moving there against his will. Lewis also opened up to Greeves often about his troubled relationship with his father. Greeves would tell Lewis about his struggles with his sickness and the goings-on in Ireland. It was through these letters where we find Lewis's innermost thoughts as he moves from atheism to a rational acceptance of theism and eventually Christianity. He allowed himself to be an open book to Greeves, and vice versa. Lewis was not ashamed to open up to Greeves about his early dabbling in sadomasochism, and Lewis was the first one to be informed when Greeves came out of the closet as a homosexual.[3] It was friendships like these, with Arthur Greeves and eventually with the Inklings, that spurred Lewis on to faith and happiness. They were the marrow in life that Lewis would enjoy, be vulnerable with, and take great delight in.

He writes to Arthur Greeves, "Friendship is the greatest of worldly good. Certainly, to me, it is the chief happiness of life. If I had to give a piece of advice to a young man about a place to live, I think I should say, 'sacrifice almost everything to live where you can be near your friends.' I know I am

3. Lewis, *Letters to Arthur*, 214.

very fortunate in that respect."[4] It was his friendships that made life worth living to Lewis. He writes in *The Four Loves*, "I have no duty to be anyone's Friend and no man in the world has a duty to be mine. No claims, no shadow of necessity. Friendship is unnecessary, like philosophy, like art, like the universe itself (for God did not need to create). It has no survival value; rather it is one of those things which give value to survival."[5] Friendships are unnecessary. One can certainly live and die after eighty years or so, having never engaged in meaningful friendships. But deep and meaningful relationships give reason and meaning to our survival. Friendships are one of the reasons we press on. They are the marrow in the bone of our existence.

I share Lewis's great love of deep and meaningful friendships. Lewis writes, "Is any pleasure on earth as great as a circle of Christian friends by a fire?"[6] I could not agree more. Great conversation, around a fire, around a coffee, around a barbeque, around a football game, around anything, has always been one of the great pleasures of my life. However, developing these friendships has routinely been a struggle of mine.

While serving in the Marines, a lot of great friendships developed naturally. They were nothing I really worked to achieve or put much thought behind. I suppose experiencing the things that we experienced together (boot camp, training schools, ship life, foreign countries, and combat) all made for friendships that developed naturally and on a sustainable level. I cherish those memories fondly.

However, when I got out and transitioned to seminary and then to professional ministry, things changed. I found friendships much harder. A lot of this has to do with my being a natural introvert, but a lot of it came from my struggle to transition from Marine mode to ministry mode. I found it harder to be myself around fellow men and women of the cloth . . . and I am assuming some found it difficult to be themselves around me. People were a lot more guarded than I was accustomed to. In the Marines I felt great freedom to be myself and was widely accepted by my peers. In professional ministry I did not feel that same freedom. It's like we all had our cards that revealed the flaws and the humanity in our lives, but rarely would one feel the comfort to show their hands. We would talk about the importance of transparency and vulnerability, but I never got to the point

4. Lewis, *Letters to Arthur*, 477.

5. Lewis, *Four Loves*, 90.

6. Lewis, *Letters of C. S. Lewis*, 467.

where I was completely real and completely myself. I had very selective transparency and vulnerability. Nevertheless, I longed for real friendships. We all do. We all long to be fully known and fully loved at the same time, as Timothy Keller would say.

It's too bad the masks we wear to match the positions we hold make vulnerability perpetually out of reach. We're afraid to show our rough side. We're afraid of being found out as a fraud. This makes us keep people out of our lives who really would know us fully and love us completely. We never give real friendship the opportunity to take root when we're not honest and transparent.

A large part of my personal problem in trying to find relationships in professional ministry was that I was trying to be friends with the very crowd that would make me put on even more of a mask. The type of friendships I was desiring were with the people who ran in the circles that I wanted to run in, groups that I wanted to be included in, and had social statuses that I wanted to be associated with. I don't think it was a coincidence that every one of the circles I wanted to run in happened to be circles that would advance my career, or at the very least, elevate me above the lower circles, which I was subconsciously convincing myself I was above. I don't think I did this on purpose. I think we all have this natural bent. We all want to be included in some sort of in-crowd. We give less attention to those whom we have a great opportunity to develop meaningful relationships with because they do nothing for us socially. What a miserable condition. I know this sounds deplorable, and I cringe as I write it, nevertheless, I have to be honest with who I was if I ever want to give God room to work in my life.

Things never had to be this way. I had a large group of people who wanted to be my friend. There were many who would have loved to know me completely and love me anyway, and for me to know them and love them back. Yet I did not take advantage. The relationships I wanted all went up on the social ladder, not down. I wasn't purposefully trying to be this arrogant and ghastly, but it sort of flowed naturally, like a lot of sin I suppose. I would never tell anyone I had little time for them, nor would I even cognitively toy with that idea. My subconscious acted on it regularly.

The friendships I was shunning early in my ministry career were not the kind of friends that you'd be excited to post a picture of on your couch for the "look at me" factor. They were what I regrettably used to call EGRs. This stands for Extra Grace Required. These were the ones who took more time out of your day than you cared to give; the ones who had issues and would love a moment of your time to discuss those issues; the ones who wanted to stand in the parking lot and talk after a long day of five church services; the ones who wanted to have a cup of coffee with you when you were too busy trying to have a cup of coffee with other staff members or with the volunteers that benefitted your ministry the most . . . the needy people who struggled with drama in their lives, struggled in their social skills, struggled in their relationships with God, and struggled with sinful habits that I had long overcome.

While I would never have said that an EGR is unworthy of my time and friendship, my life reflected it 100 percent. It showed up in who I invited over for dinner, who I tried to have conversations with in the hallways of my church, who I would post pictures of on my social media, who I would entrust with leadership positions under me.

Today, this mindset pains me. I wince when I think about my attitude, as un-purposeful as it was. I wish I could go back in time and take myself behind the woodshed for a bit. Who was I to think my time was more precious than theirs? Who was I to think that I was on some superior religious platform where I had the right to categorize them as an EGR, a little less important? Who was I? Someone who works for a church? So what? Are we not all called to ministry? Because my paycheck had the name of a church on it, did that mean I shouldn't be proud to have these struggling EGRs as my friends?

As our relationship with God grows, as we become more mature in our pursuit of him, we often find ourselves keeping those at an arm's distance who are still struggling with what we've overcome. We may engage them in ministry purposes but engaging them in vulnerable relationships is something we are prone to neglect. Lewis would have had harsh words for me back then. He would have considered me disgusting, and I cannot help but agree. In an essay published in the *Spectator* in December 1945 (now available in a collection of essays entitled *Present Concerns*) Lewis writes:

> To avoid a man's society because he is poor or ugly or stupid may be bad; but to avoid it because he is wicked—with the all but inevitable implication that you are less wicked (at least in some respect)—is dangerous and disgusting.[7]

When we separate ourselves from others because they are socially different than us: this is bad. When we separate ourselves from others because we are morally superior: this is dangerous. We are all so depraved, all so

7. Lewis, "After Priggery?," 56.

dark, and all in desperate need of grace. We are all EGRs, every last one of us, and I am in dangerous territory if I ever subconsciously believe that I do not need all the extra grace I can get. Is heaven not going to be the largest gathering of EGRs in the history of creation? Was Jesus's Parable of the Great Banquet not about inviting EGRs to share life with us? It's so easy to become what my old pastor Larry calls an accidental Pharisee.[8] It's so easy to drift away from the simple fact that we're all messed up, all on the same deplorable playfield, all in need of extra grace.

~

One author who is near to my heart is the late Henri J. M. Nouwin. He wrote several great books, but one of my favorites is a small book on Christian leadership called *In the Name of Jesus*. In it, he writes some strong words for that old version of me that subconsciously saw a divide between myself and those whom I was ministering to and leading at a church. He writes:

> Somehow we have come to believe that good leadership requires a safe distance from those we are called to lead. Medicine, psychiatry, and social work all offer us models in which "service" takes place in a one-way direction. Someone serves, someone else is being served, and be sure not to mix up the roles! But how can we lay down our life for those whom we are not even allowed to enter into a deep personal relationship?[9]

He goes on to write, "We are not the healers, we are not the reconcilers, we are not the givers of life. We are sinful, broken, vulnerable people who need as much care as anyone we care for . . . The way of the Christian leader is not the way of upward mobility in which our world has invested so much, but the way of downward mobility ending on the cross."[10] If we are serious about following Christ—that is, our lives look similar to his, and we are not fellowshipping with the marginalized, the prisoner, the immigrant, the promiscuous, the addict, the broken, and yes, even the annoying—may I be so bold to say that we are not following the model of Christ? If our social circles are not made up of those dreaded EGRs (and I mean in our social circles, not the target of our ministries, in that we actually dedicate our time and energy to sharing life with them), we are not following the model of

8. Osborne, *Accidental Pharisees.*

9. Nouwen, *In the Name,* 61.

10. Nouwen, *In the Name,* 81–82.

Christ. We may be Christians . . . that's easy to pull off. We may be religious, but we are not following the model of Jesus Christ.

One of the biggest barriers that I had to overcome in order to heal from my low spiritual self-esteem was this friendship barrier. I had to relax and accept the friendships that best cut to the core of me, no matter if I would consider them an EGR early in my ministry career. Taking a step back to survey my life now, my friends are made up of people on ends of the Extra Grace Required spectrum: EGRs who desire my attention (and I desire theirs as well); inner-city families who are so good at relationships and have taught me so much about how to be a friend; and prisoners who get my full attention, far removed from my phone, emails, and social media. I'm not trying to get anything out of them except their friendship, which is unnecessary but so rich and rewarding. I believe heaven is populated by broken people, struggling people, prisoners, and addicts at all levels of sobriety. Heaven is for those who cannot clean themselves up and needed some help. It's for those who need extra grace.

Lewis's "The Inner Ring" is an essay I have recommended to several people after I started my Lewis Remedy. It was tremendously helpful to me in understanding that I was chasing the wrong kinds of relationships for the wrong kind of reasons in my early ministry career. "The Inner Ring" helped me realize that the reason I was having a hard time developing the right kinds of relationships in my life, the kinds that I could share my deepest, innermost thoughts, was that I was trying too hard to hook my wagon to the wrong horses.

Besides being a novelist, apologist, and writer of children's fiction, Lewis was also a popular speaker. In 1944 he delivered a memorial lecture at King's College at the University of London. This lecture was entitled "The Inner Ring." Afterwards, this lecture was transcribed. It is often found today as an essay compiled in Lewis's *The Weight of Glory.* This lecture, addressed to an audience of young and aspiring college students, would be equally applicable and just as beneficial if it was given to any group of young college students today, or anyone for that matter.

In "The Inner Ring," Lewis paints a picture of something we all know exists but may struggle to describe: those inner-circles in business, at school, and at church that we all desire to be a part of—that in-crowd that we would never claim to be a part of yet are terrified of being left out of. He describes the ring itself as not being a bad thing necessarily—indeed, how would one ever be friends with one person if they were friends with everyone, or how could a business ever run sufficiently if everyone, at all times, got to be a part of every decision that was made? It is the *desire* to be in the Inner Ring, however, that can bring about some potentially catastrophic results. The desire will not only be catastrophic personally, but also to the organization that one is a part of. Lewis writes, "Unless you take measurements to prevent it, this desire is going to be one of the chief motives of your life, from the first day on which you enter your profession until the day when you are too old to care."[11] When the desire to be within the Inner Ring of any organization of people is one's chief motivation, that person will never quite have the impact that he or she desires. The mission of that organization will always come in second. One's status will mean more than one's impact. This is unhealthy for everyone involved.

Lewis gives two specific reasons why a desire to be counted among the Inner Ring is harmful. For one, he writes, "Of all the passions, the passion for the Inner-Ring is most skillful in making a man who is not yet a very bad man do very bad things," and two, "As long as you are governed by that desire you will never get what you want. You are trying to peel an onion; if you succeed there will be nothing left. Until you conquer the fear of being an outsider, an outsider you will remain."[12] When people are governed by the fear of being left out of the inner-circle, they will remain on the outside forever, and perhaps do some pretty shady things along the way.

Our desire to be friends with only those in an Inner Ring keeps us in a perpetual place of feeling alone. We keep all potential real friends at an arm's distance while chasing an outcome that will never be. Those who desire to be in the Inner Ring, and operate out of that desire, will never feel that they have reached the inside. This is a lonely position to be in indeed.

I always felt sorry for that little mouse running in his wheel. I always wondered if he knew he wasn't going anywhere, no matter how hard he tried. Perhaps he just wanted some exercise, but perhaps he thought he was traveling a great distance, only to end up in the exact same place. My desire to be accepted by only those whose acceptance I longed for was keeping me on an unending wheel of loneliness. Lewis goes on to remind me that the quest for the Inner Ring will break my heart, because I will be chasing a status that does not really exist. Most people do not realize that they are in an Inner Ring, so those desiring it will be chasing a ghost. They will be a perpetual mouse on the wheel.

11. Lewis, "Inner Ring," 152.
12. Lewis, "Inner Ring," 154.

We all know those types of people. We all know those types of people whose work is not their end. Getting noticed is their end. Being at the right parties is their end. Being invited into the right kinds of meetings is their end. Having a beer with the boss after work is their end. Exchanging a lower title for a higher title is their end . . . the Dwight Schrutes of the world who quietly change their title from "Assistant to the General Manager" to "Assistant Manager." Most have had experience with these types of personalities, and most people do not find them very attractive. They seem weak and petty. While there are many words that can describe them, confident is not one of them. Their insecurities are the armpit stains that everyone at the workplace can see but them. These people are who the quest for the Inner Ring is destroying.

But for those whose work is their end, i.e., desiring excellence in their work, they are going to wake up and find themselves in an interesting position. If someone focuses simply on the task at hand, if they put their head down and work hard rather than keep their head up and try to advance themselves, they are going to stumble into some surprising results. These people are, as Lewis describes them, craftsmen—those who are exceptional at their particular trade. They are not worried about the promotion so much as they are worried about blooming where they are planted. They are not worried about status so much as they are worried about their competency. They do not want to be found at the best parties so much as they want to be found at being the best at what they do. Excellence is their goal, not simply being perceived as excellent.

Not only will these craftsmen be more competent and reliable than the sweat-stained Dwight Schrutes among us, something else will occur. After long periods of simply putting one's head down and working hard to be the best they can be, other sound craftsmen will be attracted to them. They will begin to relate to others at the same motivation and skill level. Their passion for their craft, and not their passion for status, will be the glue that binds them. They will find great commonality in their skill levels. They will get together after work to talk about their trade. Other people will approach this group of friends because they evidently know what they are doing when it comes to that particular craft. Some may be better than others, but the interest levels are all the same. Although they will not recognize it as such, one day they will raise their head to realize they are very much in the middle of something that looks an awful lot like an Inner Ring—but it would have happened organically, or as Lewis puts it, accidently. And this group of craftsmen, whose passion is stirred for each other not because it moves them up the chain but because of their similarities, will realize they have something far better than an Inner Ring. They will be friends. They will be real friends, for the simple sake of being friends. This type of friendship, Lewis writes, "causes perhaps half of all the happiness in the world, and no Inner Ring can ever have it."[13]

Once again, Lewis brought my struggles back to one unavoidable conclusion: my eyes were still on me. Not on others. Not on my mission. Not on God. My struggle to make and maintain deep friendship was boiling down to pride, as many struggles in this life tend to do. I wanted friendships, but I wanted them because they looked like an Inner Ring, and that desire sacrificed some potentially beautiful friendships along the way. I had wasted so much time and passed on so many great would-be friendships because my motivations were off. Lewis helped me realize this.

"The Inner Ring," if one allows it, will call out these prideful motivations in just about anyone that reads it. And I read it and internalized it. I put my head down. I went to work and gave little thought to my status. When I moved on to my next area of ministry, I opened my heart to relationships with everyone. They looked very different than the relationships I was chasing before. I invited people over to barbeque whom I would have previously considered an EGR. I made friends with those I worked with in the inner-city and in prison, with no thought to how their friendships would benefit me, or if I would feel important because of them. I didn't worry about relationships "draining" me. I looked for ways that those relationships could fulfill me. I focused on being a good friend. I focused on others. I forgot about me, as often as I could. I'm not sure if I am in any Inner Ring today, but I sure do not care one way or another. I have great friends. They know the real me and I know the real them. They know my dirt and I know their dirt, and we love each other regardless. These kinds of relationships will never be shaken by a superficial desire for an Inner Ring.

"The Inner Ring" illuminated an inner struggle I carried for so long. Just like any condition, once the causes were exposed, it was much easier to move away from it. When I have been tempted to get down because I see a relationship, or a group of relationships, that I want to be a part of and it is seemingly not rolling out the welcome mat, I ask myself, "Is this an Inner Ring that I want to be a part of because they are an Inner Ring, or do I truly desire a relationship with them because I can be vulnerable and real with them?" Many times, the answer is it's just another Inner Ring, and that's the real allure of the would-be friendships. Once identified and called out for

13. Lewis, "Inner Ring," 156–57.

what it is, I can move on and seek the relationships that truly allow me to be me.

Some people spend their whole lives trying to work for the best companies, the best churches, the best organizations . . . whatever "best" means anyway. They spend their whole lives trying to work up the corporate ladders or work themselves into those elite rings, filled with the powerful, the rich, the people in control, and the people in the know. Lewis taught me to relax. To bloom where I am planted. To focus on others and on the mission. To focus on God.

While this still may be a dragon to slay every once a while, the results have been tremendous. Deep and abiding friendships are worth their weight in gold, silver, or any other precious jewel. If anyone is without the kind of relationship where one can relax, laugh, be flawed, and enjoy one another, I could not recommend that they fix this faster. It is one of the best ways to pull one out of low spiritual self-esteem, and indeed keep them out.

The Eagle and Child reminded us of the importance of making friends who we can simply have fun with, with no expectations of elevating anything but one another's laughter. It reminds us that real friendships happen over common interests and experiences, and nothing else. Anything else is fool's gold, all the way through, no matter how beautiful it may appear. Following Jesus may end on a cross, so it's important to share some laughs and memories with some great friends along the way, no matter what those relationships do for one's career or social status.

I don't think it's any coincidence that Jesus's first miracle was not raising the dead, or walking on water, it was simply making wine at a party . . . the best wine they had ever tasted. Christ's first miracle was extremely social in nature. It was simple, no matter how much the theologians have attempted to complicate it. Jesus' first miracle was giving his friends wine at a celebration. Friendships are what make life worth enjoying. Like the bells and whistles on the higher trims of a car line, they are not needed but certainly do add a level of comfort. Healthy friendships are a crucial preventative maintenance tool to add to one's toolbox. This is one of the ways Lewis has helped me grow the quality of the life that God has blessed me with. I pray the reader is blessed with that too.

15

Comparison Is of Hell

The desire for fame appears to me as a competitive passion and therefore of hell rather than heaven.

—C. S. LEWIS, *THE WEIGHT OF GLORY*[1]

THE unfortunate tendency to compare myself to other Christians has always been a regular supplier of low spiritual self-esteem . . . and one I was happy to abandon. It took a while to get there, however. I would see other Christians living the seemingly wholesome life I desired. I would see healthy, intact families who were the poster child of a happy midwestern Christian family unit attending church together. I would hear the pastors I respected describe their lives, habits, and families as something, I perceived, to be nearly perfect. Even the areas they would describe as troublesome were so trivial compared to mine. A pastor, whom I greatly respect, once told a story about a time years ago when he said a pretty bad curse word, and how deeply ashamed of it he was. He was deeply ashamed of this curse word that resided below the surface and came out upon an intense shock of pain. I imagine it took a great deal of courage for him to be honest with his congregation about it. I admire him for being honest with his church about his flaws, which he often does. But I could not help but think that if every time I have ever slipped and let a bad word come out of my mouth. If I was as distraught as he was every time I let a curse word slip, I would never get off the ground in shame.

1. Lewis, "The Weight of Glory," 36.

My life would be made up of sackcloth and ashes. Yet this was the moment that my pastor, who in my mind set the standard for God-pleasing spirituality, wished he could go back in time and erase. I was so far gone compared to him. When I heard his story I was in the process of an ugly divorce. *I wonder if this pastor has ever gone through that . . .* comparison.

I see a successful couple at church who have been married for years. They have five kids and are adopting their sixth from Rwanda. Then I go home to manage my single parent household and try not to think, *how many divorced, single-parent pastors do I know? Not many.* Of course, the answer to this question is probably several, but the oppressing comparison trap does not free my mind to consider this. Then I feel sorry for myself. Then I ask myself where I went wrong. Then I allow my thoughts, my remorse, and my actions to focus back on one singular topic: me. Comparison once again leads me back to me. Comparison, once again, leads me back to pride—thinking of myself instead of others . . . instead of God.

There is nothing good that can ever come from comparing ourselves to anyone. It will lead to pride every time, even if it is the sneaky kind of pride that disguises itself as inwardly focused self-remorse. I can see why "Thou shalt not covet" made the Old Testament Top Ten List . . . it can only lead to comparison. Is it any wonder why comparison is "of hell"? It is a breeding ground for lies and an offramp for prideful depression. Ripping the comparison trap out of my life was one of the most beneficial steps I have made towards combating my low spiritual self-esteem, and it still must be done daily.

Lewis did not believe in comparisons. He believed there was nothing good that could come from comparing yourself to another. Comparing yourself to someone you look up to is just as harmful and egotistical as comparing yourself to someone you look down on. Comparing oneself, on any level, to anyone, either inwardly or outwardly, can be extremely damaging. Lewis writes, "Pride gets no pleasure out of having something, only out of having more of it than the next man . . . It is the comparison that makes you proud: the pleasure of being above the rest."[2] Pride, as mentioned earlier, is the worst of all sins, which makes comparison the gateway-drug to avoid at all costs, no matter which side effect it leads to. Screwtape wants people comparing. One side effect of comparison could be low spiritual self-esteem like

2. Lewis, *Mere Christianity*, 122.

me, or another on the opposite end: extreme pride. What other outcome is there? Either side effect is a dreadful one to achieve indeed.

Lewis says that we can never really know what someone is actually like on the inside. We will never know of their temptations, their opportunities, or their struggles. "One soul in the whole of creation you do know: and it is the only one whose fate is placed in your hands."[3] To what then is there to compare? Scripture is clear that everyone is fallen and that everyone is in desperate need of his grace.[4] So to whom do we compare?

Lewis would remind us that we simply do not know where others are struggling, but we can rest assured they are. Writing to friend Sheldon Vanauken, in December 1950, he inquires, "Have you read the Analects of Confucius? He ends up by saying 'This is the Tao. I do not know if anyone has ever kept it.' That's significant: one can really go direct from there to the Epistle of the Romans."[5] The Tao, which Lewis is borrowing from Chinese culture, refers to natural law, traditional morality, and the sole source of all value judgments.[6] Here, Lewis is agreeing that no person has ever kept the Tao . . . not one.

We say that no one is perfect, but we never live in that. Our lives never relax in that. We agree that no one is perfect, but we fight and we claw and we cry and we kick and scream as if perfection is obtainable. Yet, we are so far from where perfection would have us. Not only do we often fail to live by societal laws and God's laws, we do not even live by our own laws. When one can internalize the fact that not one person is able to keep even the law written on their very own hearts, and live in that internalization practically, it frees one from the damaging prisons of comparison. It levels the playing field and moves everyone to the same sinful platform, leaving all in need of a savior. When everyone is on the same playing field, comparison proves useless.

A Christ-follower who is a struggling alcoholic is no nearer to God than one who is a struggling workaholic. A Christian whose flaws include intense lust over another person is on the same level as a pastor who is lustful of the attendance of the church down the road. Both are at the same starting point with God. Both are in need of the same grace . . . the same death on the cross. "It is the comparison that makes you proud: the pleasure of being above the rest. Once the element of competition is gone, pride is gone."[7]

3. Lewis, *Mere Christianity*, 216–17.

4. Rom 3:23.

5. Lewis, *Yours, Jack*, 154.

6. Lewis, *Abolition of Man*, 55.

7. Lewis, *Mere Christianity*, 122.

And with pride leaving, so does any chance of low spiritual self-esteem. We need to drop the competition. There is no competition. If we can get rid of all pride, we will get rid of all competition. If we can get rid of all competition, we will get rid of all pride.

Lewis writes, "When Christ died, He died for you individually just as much as if you had been the only person in the world."[8] With that kind of individual attention, where does comparison find a foothold? We are all naked and afraid. All vulnerable. All dirty. Yet Christ died for each and every one of us, as if there was no one else to die for. Where do we find any sort of pride above the rest?

C. S. Lewis, over the course of these three years of my life, continued to help me conquer my battle against low spiritual self-esteem. Like a good counselor sitting between two spouses at domestic war with one another, Lewis was reintroducing me to how much I loved God. It was interesting though . . . it felt as if my view of the divine was returning to its proper place, although I cannot recall ever having this robust view of God. It felt like I returned home though I did not recall ever being there before. I felt lighter.

Remedial actions are anything that we do immediately the moment something goes wrong. Growing up with asthma, besides performing all of the preventative maintenance steps along the way, such as sleeping with a humidifier and staying away from tobacco, a corrective action was to keep an inhaler in my pocket to shoot into my pipes the moment I felt discomfort in my lungs.

In the military, remedial actions are immediate actions taken the moment a piece of equipment stops functioning. If a weapon stops firing in the middle of a firefight, there are several steps to perform in order the get the it functioning again. The goal is for the remedial action to happen so quick and so naturally that the soldier or Marine does not have to think about it. It is just a matter of muscle memory. Remedial actions are the first steps to take the moment anything goes wrong.

My journey with Lewis taught me a few remedial actions to take or principles to remember the moment I made a mistake or felt myself drifting in my relationship with God. I will cover a few of these in the next section.

8. Lewis, *Mere Christianity*, 168.

PART 5

Essays on Remedial Actions

16

Try Again

But the great thing to remember is that, though our feelings come and go, His love for us does not. It is not wearied by our sins, or our indifference; and, therefore, it is quite relentless in its determination that we shall be cured of those sins, at whatever cost to us, at whatever cost to Him.

—C. S. LEWIS, *MERE CHRISTIANITY*[1]

As previously mentioned, out of all the sources of my low spiritual self-esteem, the biggest and undoubtedly most frequent source has always been my recurring mistakes. They have special power to make me relapse. They have the power to make me give up. They have the power to make me believe I am a third-string Christian. They scare me. It always made sense to me that God could forgive a one or two failures, but my view of God was never big enough to consider that he could forgive repeated mistakes.

For Christians like me, the cycle is the same. We go through the motions. We mess up again, often the same screw up we have asked forgiveness for before. We say our prayers. We legitimately feel sorry. Yet simultaneously we stand up, walk away, and are assured that God is not going to stand for our recurring failures . . . not the same ones we have been asking forgiveness for.

My false view of God's intolerance of my repeated mistakes is extremely harmful to my spiritual health. I need to be on the guard of this

---

1. Lewis, *Mere Christianity*, 99.

feeling that will surely make me relapse back into my low spiritual condition when the next repeated failure resurfaces. I need someone I trust to help me remember that I am never out of the fight, that as long as we have a sinful nature, the battle will rage. Lewis helps. He writes:

> After each failure, ask forgiveness, pick yourself up, and try again . . . The only thing fatal is to sit down, content with anything less than perfection.[2]

I remember reading these words of Lewis with this issue of recurring sins far from my mind. I was reading out of pure enjoyment. However, this hit me with a left jab that I was not expecting. I remember folding the book down and trying to breathe this in. Tears about to drop, I thought there was hope for this battered soul. My microscopic view of God and his love was once again going to be shattered, rebuilt, and made much larger. Out of all my repeated failures, one thing that I had never done was sit down, "content with anything less than perfection." I was always able to try again, yet the mere fact that I was "trying again" made me feel like a spiritual loser, not an attribute to be proud of.

For the longest time, I had been an expert at trying again. I had plenty of practice. Yet, the disconnect for me was that I was convinced that God's forgiveness would eventually end. I would never say that, but I would live in it practically. Yet here Lewis is making the point that God's greatest desire for me may be to learn the virtue of trying again. Trying again is actually a virtue in itself, a virtue that I finally started thinking God may be proud of me for having. It had been a long time since I thought God could be proud of me for anything. Sober-mindedness is important, just as courage, truthfulness, charity, fairness, unselfishness, and any other virtue. But God's highest virtue for me in this current stage of my Christian journey might be simply the ability to try again, continue to rely on him, and continue to rely on his forgiveness. When one has a colossal failure, God's best for that person might simply be to try again . . . I could do that.

Lewis says that trying again cures our illusion of ourselves. As I mentioned earlier, a regular source of my undesirable condition came from my mistakes crashing my high expectations of myself. My illusions of myself, and the perfection I was subconsciously demanding, needed to be cured. This did not mean I needed to develop low expectations of myself—of course not. It meant achieving a more accurate view of my humanity.

Lewis was not teaching Christians to set the bar low, not in the least bit; indeed, we are not to be "content with anything less that perfection." He

---

2. Lewis, *Mere Christianity*, 101.

was reminding Christ-followers to keep pushing forward, to not let our sinful humanity get us down, to stay reliant on God's grace and not dependent on ourselves. Again, it seemed that when dealing with our mistakes, the weight isn't on our ability to fail or not fail, to abstain or not abstain. No, what it boils down to is the Christian's ability to trust God, amidst his or her sinful humanity . . . to keep charging forward . . . to be found in the resistance . . . to trust him and not one's own ability. Why do so many of us Christians have the ever-present desire to make everything about us? About our ability to perform or not to perform? To sin or not to sin? Sometimes I believe God looks down at us and shakes his head, thinking *I took care of your sinful nature two thousand years ago. Why are you still concerned with it? Drop the drama already and relax in me.*

After being immersed in Lewis for these three years or so, I've begun to think perhaps I am closer to where God wants me to be than I realize, flaws and all, because after all, he will not judge us as if we have no difficulties to overcome.[3] Lewis reminds me, "No amount of fails will really undo us if we keep picking ourselves up each time. We shall of course be very muddy and tattered children by the time we reach home. But the bathrooms are all ready, the towels put out . . . The only fatal thing is to lose one's temper and give up."[4] In case of a spiritual relapse, Lewis helps me to learn that I am never out of the fight. What a great thought. We can be equally as virtuous as the next guy, simply by trying again.

The quote that began this chapter from *Mere Christianity* certainly rises to the top of my favorite Lewis lines. Our feelings ebb and flow. They are affected by our surrounding circumstances, our past experiences, our exercise, our lack of exercise, heredity, biology, neurology, and diet. Our feelings come and go. God's love for us does not come and go. It is more consistent than the ever-changing neurons bouncing around in our brains. God is not wearied by our mistakes. He does not grow tired of our indifference. Indeed, he is relentless in his determination to rid us of those mistakes, no matter what it costs us and no matter what it costs him. He proved that relentlessness on the cross. Take heart. His relentlessness will outlast humanity's most recurring and horrendous of blunders.

3. Lewis, *Mere Christianity*, 99.
4. Lewis, *Letters of C. S. Lewis*, 470.

17

Thickening Is a Process

the trouble is that relying on God has to begin all over again every day as if nothing had yet been done.

—C. S. Lewis, a letter written to Mrs. Lockley, September 1949[1]

WE will not reach the platform of perfection anytime soon. As far as Lewis is concerned, our spiritual journey is one of going further up and further in over a period of eternity.[2] Every day we can take small steps towards a journey of thickening, leaving behind the evil, and adding the good. This is, according to Lewis, a journey that will even continue after death.

In *The Great Divorce*, "thickening" is a process,[3] even in the afterlife. The ghost tourists from hell were out of their element. The outskirts of heaven, where their bus was parked, was not a friendly environment as their translucent bodies were weak and scared. They couldn't lift a single leaf. They could not even bear to step on the blades of grass as the pain was sharp and penetrating. Yet if they chose to stay, and chose full surrender to God, they would begin to thicken. They would grow hard feet just like the heavenly spirits that hosted them, as they began their journeys into the mountains of God, going further up and further in, growing closer to their Creator every step of the way. For Lewis, our steps toward perfection and

1. Lewis, *Letters of C. S. Lewis*, 507.
2. Lewis, *Last Battle*, 201.
3. Lewis, *Great Divorce*, 99.

our quest to shed our humanity are processes that begin here in the Shadowlands but will be stretched well into eternity.

As we live our lives on earth, we are already on our eternal journey. For those who make earth their goal, instead of Heaven, they are already living in a region of Hell, and their journey will continue until they choose otherwise. For those who choose Heaven will find that they are in the beginning stages of Heaven itself, and the journey will continue well into the next life . . . the real life[4].

I find comfort to know that, even on the other side of eternity, we've still got some "thickening up" to do. I'm not sure why that brings me comfort. I guess because I feel so very far away from perfection right now. If I showed up to heaven as I write this, I would feel naked, embarrassed, and not ready. However, if God zapped me and removed my sinful nature automatically, like I guess we assume he's going to do, I would be a completely different person, oblivious to the mistake-prone nature that I just had up until a moment ago. I would snap into conformity. Snap into cleanliness. I would be zapped far away from my original personality and zapped into whatever the zapper preferred me to be. I would be zapped into . . . well, not far removed from that of a robot.

Yet, if it was a journey that I had to overcome, still shedding the parts of my being that I did not want in the presence of God, allowing him to bring to attention that which is wrong and that which I still needed to surrender to him, I would feel much more at peace with the transition. Even on the other side of eternity. It would be much more personal. It would be real. It would be a tangible change that happened because my germ of a desire for God exploded into wholehearted mission to get closer to him. It would not be God zapping me into a different personality. It would be me offering parts of my personality up to God and allowing him to make the necessary changes.

Lewis believes that this is the original idea of the doctrine of purgatory, or at least something like it. No matter what the Christian believes about purgatory, or if it fits with one's denominational preferences, Lewis does make a good point that we do in fact demand some kind of cleaning up process. Our souls demand some kind of thickening treatment that begins here and ends somewhere on the other side, deep in the eternal mountains of God.

In *Letters to Malcom: Chiefly on Prayer* he writes that our souls insist on some kind of purgatory or expunging. He made the point that it would break our hearts for God to tell us that we are dirty, we smell, and our clothes

4. Lewis, *Great Divorce*, IX.

are tattered, but we are nevertheless welcome. No one here will judge us or attempt to clean us up. Would we feel excited about the joy we are about to enter knowing that there has not been some purging of our diabolical self along the way? Would we prefer to enter into eternity the way we are? Would we not reply, "'With submissions, sir, and if there is no objection, I'd rather be cleaned first?'

'It may hurt, you know.'

'Even so, sir.'"[5]

We would not want to be zapped into submission, would we? Would the college student want the degree without having sweated and triumphed over the exams? Would the soldier want to be granted that title without having first gone through boot camp? Don't get me wrong. This has nothing to do with earning. It has everything to do with purging . . . and there's a reason why this should be of value to us.

Lewis believes in this so much that he even prays for the dead as they continue on their journey.[6] Wayne Martin Dale writes about Lewis, "Of course, he couldn't pray for them nor would the prayers be beneficial if they were already perfected in Heaven."[7] Lewis is still rooting for their purification journey in paradise!

The reason that the idea of some kind of purging should be good news is that the more darkness we leave behind now, the more distance we can make on our journey of going further into the things of God, and thus the closer we get to ultimate joy and fulfillment. We can actually start the journey right now. We can go further up and further in on this side of eternity. Thickening is a process that we can begin immediately.

This should be great news as our soul takes three steps forward and two back. Every day we go further up and further in, inching our way through a process that will extend on the other side of heaven. That should be a comfort to us. It seems it extends our deadline in a sense (not that it has an effect on where we spend eternity), but in another sense it also means that we can move along quite far in our journey here and now. Our souls demand purgatory? Well, let us start the process now.

5. Lewis, *Letters to Malcom,* 108–9.

6. Lewis, *Letters to Malcom,* 120.

7. Martindale, *Beyond Shadowlands,* 201.

18

Misguided Attempts at Redemption

every sin is the distortion of an energy breathed into us—an energy which, if not thus distorted, would have blossomed into one of those holy acts whereof "God did it" and "I did it" are both true descriptions.

—C. S. LEWIS, *LETTERS TO MALCOM*[1]

WHAT are our mistakes? Why the crimes? Why the rebellion? What are we indeed searching for? What are we trying to accomplish? Lewis would argue that we are trying to achieve redemption. It may be misguided. It may be, of course. It may be severely corrupted, but it is an attempt at redemption, nonetheless. Lewis would say that our mistakes are never us being bad for the simple sake of being bad. Our mistakes are misplaced goodness. They are missing the real mark of what we were really aiming at. It is like a Marine on the rifle range grabbing a Nerf gun instead of his M-16. His intentions are correct. He will have a gun in his hands but in no way will he ever hit the target. It will be a poor excuse for the real thing. We are misfiring every day, forgetting the source of our joy and the freedom found therein. In *The Pilgrim's Regress* Lewis writes, "What does not satisfy when we find it, was not the thing we were desiring."[2] Does a crooked investor ever feel complete satisfaction after swindling his clients out of hoards of money? Does the dad who left his family for another woman ever feel whole afterwards? Does the

1. Lewis, *Letters to Malcom*, 69.
2. Lewis, *Pilgrim's Regress*, 128.

overbearing boss who beat his employees' morale down to submission ever feel fulfilled for doing so? Does the addict ever feel a sense of security and wholeness when she is abusing drugs or alcohol? Does the tax-cheat, homewrecker, fraudster, liar, or abuser ever feel sheer satisfaction and fulfillment after committing their trespass? The answer to all of the questions is an obvious no. So why the violations? They are all looking for redemption.

University Church of St. Mary the Virgin

As we strolled down the streets of Oxford one day, our professor led us into a church that looked as if it had been there for quite some time . . . and it had. Some parts of the building had been there since the 1200s. We walked into the University Church of St. Mary the Virgin, off of High Street in downtown Oxford, unaware of all the history that had taken place there. This church was center point where the University of Oxford grew. This was where the famous Oxford Martyrs were tried before they were burnt at the stake just north of where we stood. This was where John Wesley not only attended church but eventually preached in the mid-1700s. I could go on and on about the history that had taken place long before we graced the arched doorways.

I love all things history. I love visiting historic sights. So naturally it was a surreal moment for me as I approached the stairs that circled around a pillar, leading up to a pulpit that was perched about ten feet off the ground. This was where the sermons were given. This is where the current priests still deliver their messages to their faithful flock at Oxford. It was off-centered. It was actually placed noticeably to the far right of the sanctuary, from the onlooker's perspective. This was done on purpose. The speaker was never supposed to be the focal point of the room.

My favorite part of that pulpit, however, was that this was where C. S. Lewis delivered one of his most beloved lectures, *The Weight of Glory*. The manuscript has since been made into one of his most powerful books, in this author's opinion. I typically advise anyone interested in getting into Lewis to start with *The Weight of Glory*. Here I was, in the exact location where it was delivered. Tourists snapped their pictures around me. Someone knelt to pray in the pews behind me. A couple held hands, leaning over the balcony above me. I crossed my arms and stared at that historic pulpit above me:

> There are no *ordinary* people. You have never talked to a mere mortal. Nations, cultures, arts, civilization—these are mortal,

and their life is to ours as the life of a gnat. But it is immortals whom we joke with, work with, marry, snub, and exploit . . . Next to the Blessed Sacrament itself, your neighbor is the holiest object presented to your senses.[3]

I was staring at that spot where Lewis's thick Irish accent bellowed those lines to a packed house of Oxford students several decades ago. There were just as many students standing as there were sitting due to lack of space. It was from this pulpit that Lewis would articulate so precisely what my heart needed to hear decades later. Here he told me that all my mistakes, and the sin that weighted on me so heavily, were the product of longing for peace with God but searching for that peace in all the wrong areas.

We all have a deep longing in us that no earthly experience can satisfy. Lewis says that we call it nostalgia, romance, or adolescence, but we're far off. All the beauty we seek out and enjoy in this life is but a small taste of the beauty we are actually longing for. We see a painting, hear a song, smell a flower, and we may absorb all the beauty possible within that experience, but we will still be longing for more. Here, in this ancient church at Oxford, Lewis proclaimed that the books and music that we enjoy, everything that we find beautiful today, will deceive us if we trust them. We are not truly longing for these things, as beautiful and desirable as they may be. We are longing for something much grander. They are simply false conduits. The art we enjoy, the relationships we long for, and even the nostalgia of our own past are not the real objects of our desires but just the hint of the real object. Be fooled no longer. All of these things may be good, but they are "only the scent of a flower we have not found, the echo of a tune we have not heard, news from a country we have never yet visited."[4] This was the spot where Lewis proclaimed those marvelous insights.

In *The Weight of Glory*, Lewis reminds us that we all have a deep longing. We all have a desire for joy. We all want to not only see and hear beauty but become part of it. When we see a beautiful painting that captures our attention, we are not only marveling at the skill of the artist, we are desiring to be consumed by its beauty. When we hear a piece of music that touches our soul, we are not only impressed by makeup of the song, we want to fall into it. We want to become one with it. We get to the edge of beauty and to the edge of where our human experience allows us to go, and we want more. We are starved for more beauty. We are starved for more wholeness.

All of our attempts to find something lovely in this world are all attempts to get back to a place we have never been, but our hearts remember

---

3. Lewis, "Weight of Glory," 46.
4. Lewis, "Weight of Glory," 39–40.

as if we have. All of our attempts at finding beauty are all longings for heaven, yearnings to be in perfect union with our Creator. We've all been cut off from paradise. We've all been alienated from the one sustaining force in this life we were created to be fulfilled by. We've all been removed from a relationship with God, and we're all desperately trying to get back to the security, the beauty, the meaning, and the redemption that comes with union with him . . . whether we know it or not . . . whether we believe in God or not . . . mankind is in desperate search for him.

That's what our mistakes are: misguided attempts at redemption. We're trying to recreate that feeling of wholeness that our hearts remember but our body has never experienced. When we abuse drugs or alcohol, we do it to escape. We're tired of this world and how it presents itself, and we're tired of the toxic emotions that it conjures. The euphoric mindset that substance abuse brings about is chased to get to a world where there will be no more mourning, no more tears, no more death. When we lie it is typically to feel reassured in ourselves or our situations—to make others approve of us and accept us. Perhaps we are all striving for that form of self-assurance that we know exists but can't seem to achieve on our own. We know we should be self-assured, meaning that complete self-assurance does in fact exist, so we fumble our way through life trying to find it. Perhaps we are starving for that approval that will come only, once and for all, when we hear the words, "Well done my good and faithful servant."[5] When we hoard money, perhaps we are yearning for a security that we all know is simply not possible in this life but we assume is achievable. Perhaps we're looking for a security that only comes when we enter a reality where our treasure does not rust and where moths do not eat.[6]

I was standing in the spot where Lewis had called my bluff. I sat down on one of the pews and began to think about the sin in my life, all the mistakes I had made, and the repeated, nearly habitual failures that had been so damaging to my relationship with God and my own spiritual self-esteem. While I always remain deeply remorseful about my mistakes, indeed probably too remorseful at times, for some reason it helped just a little bit to realize that my mistakes were misfires at a real joy and a real intimacy that does in fact exist, and one that I will have one day. This isn't to excuse the sin in our lives. It must be weeded out, as much as it can be. We must be found in the resistance, but Lewis helped me understand my heart a little more, and the little I did know about my heart reminded me that I do not desire evil. I do not desire to do wrong. My desire is for Christ. My desire

5. Matt 25:2.
6. Matt 6:19.

is redemption. My desire is to be made whole. Whether I hit the target or not, my inner being has been aiming at Christ. If Lewis could decode my heart, even just that much, if I could sit there in that pew at the University Church in Oxford and understand my heart a little more than I had the day before, then could I not relax a little and trust that the God whom I trust with my very existence knows the depths and the secrets of my heart and true desires, more so than I could ever dare dream?

Lewis says in *The Weight of Glory*, "It would seem that Our Lord finds our desires not too strong, but too weak . . . we are far too easily pleased."[7] We have a deep desire for something else, for something more significant. We have a deep longing for true beauty and to be made whole, yet these long- ings are often materialized into small, pesky misfires. These are misfires that are often directed at joy but get lost along the way. We go about fooling with drink and sex and ambition,[8] for example, expecting them to satisfy, not realizing that they are poor substitutes for oneness with our Creator, which is what we're all thirsting for. Not that our substitutes are always bad; indeed, God created all the great pleasures and wants us to enjoy them as they were created. But the pleasures that can so easily become our goal are meant to simply enhance our journey, not consume it. When our pursuit is only to- wards the pleasures and not Christ, we're going to miss joy every time. Our souls wither without Christ. God is the only endeavor in life that is meant to satisfy. There is nothing else in existence that satisfies. There is no other stream.[9] Identifying our mistakes for what they really are, longings for our heart's desire, is crucial towards maintaining any sort of spiritual health. True redemption is out there, and it one day will complete us, but in the meantime may we turn our search for redemption to a search for him. May we enjoy the echoes and the scents of that true beauty along the way and allow it to fuel our passion for the one day when we will fall into the art. We will be encompassed in the beautiful. We will be redeemed.

7. Lewis, "Weight of Glory," 26.

8. Lewis, *Surprised by Joy,* 170.

9. Lewis, *Silver Chair*, 23.

19

Sincerity and Perseverance

If you are on the wrong road, progress means doing an about-turn and walking back to the right road.

—C. S. Lewis, Mere Christianity[1]

O NE of the most important lessons Lewis teaches me through all of this is to pace myself and focus on one victory today, and then perhaps another tomorrow. Christ tells us to pick up our cross daily and follow him.[2] He does not say, "Pick up your cross one time and get to where you're going. Oh, and be sure not to drop it along the way." It is a daily process. One might have picked up their cross years ago at a church summer camp, but that cross must indeed need to be picked up every waking morning from then on, especially when the road gets bumpy and one might drop it. Regarding any habitual or recurring mistake in the Christian's life, Lewis writes in *Mere Christianity*, "God knows our situation; he will not judge us as if we had no difficulties to overcome. What matters is the sincerity and perseverance of our will to overcome them."[3] Following Christ is a daily event. Just like any relationship, it takes a renewed commitment every day to make the relationship work.

It is so easy for us to look at where we want to be, look at where we are, and fall into a spiritual depression, especially if we are prone to comparison.

1. Lewis, *Mere Christianity*, 28.
2. Luke 9:23.
3. Lewis, *Mere Christianity*, 99.

We do not realize that where we want to be someday is a matter of taking small steps towards that today. We just look at the great distance between here and there, drop our shoulders, and give up.

"Do not worry about tomorrow. Tomorrow will worry about itself."[4] We have to learn to stop looking at the big picture and what total victory will look like and focus on our small manageable victories today. The big picture can often be overwhelming to someone who wants severe change. It is daunting and unmanageable. Yet today is much more manageable. As I mentioned before there was a period of my life that I abused alcohol. To stop abusing alcohol I did not just stop being an alcoholic. I stopped being an alcoholic for one day. Then I did it again the next day. The following day I might fail, but I decided to not let that worry me today. I just stopped abusing alcohol for one day. Eventually, my one day of victory, with some failures along the way, became two days of victories in a row. Then three. Then four.

Lewis writes in *Mere Christianity*, "Very often what God first helps us towards is not the virtue itself but just this power of always trying again."[5] God's best place for us may not be the virtue of courage or truthfulness or charity. God's best place for us might simply be trying today to be virtuous, courageous, or charitable. If a woman is prone to being prideful and she wants to change, perhaps her biggest victory would not be to become completely free of all pride. Maybe her biggest victory, and the one that would make God equally proud, is to go one day without boasting or making a prideful comment. If a man is prone to being a workaholic, instead of looking at the end goal of becoming completely free from his addiction, perhaps the best way for him to serve God, and himself for that matter, is to go one day or one evening without doing any work when he is desperately tempted to do so. God may be just as proud of the drug addict who goes one day without using as the man who spends his entire life drug free. Indeed, both will make the Father proud.

I once got to learn something about the power of small victories and using those victories as fuel to press on. I was an infantry instructor in the Marine Corps. My fellow instructors and I would take one class of Marines per week and put them through a rigorous course called Combat Skills Training School. All of us instructors were infantry Marines, had served at least one four-year enlistment before coming to be an instructor, and were

4. Matt 6:34.
5. Lewis, *Mere Christianity*, 101.

combat experienced. Our students however, while all Marines, had jobs in the Corps that were non-combative. We had Marines who drove trucks, delivered mail, worked on computers, etc. But with any job in the Marine Corps, especially while engaging in the War on Terror, every soldier, sailor, and Marine could find themselves in a position where they would have to fight their way through. So, we made sure our students were pushed—and pushed hard. Many of them would deploy soon after our course.

At the end of this grueling week of intense infantry training in the field—eating, sleeping, and working through all of nature's elements—we would take our students on a motivation hike, up and down some mountains in Southern California. It was a hard hike, and we kept our students marching at a pretty fast pace. Many times, their gear was wet for a week from the weather and the streams and rivers around our camp. Many of them had more gear on than they were used to carrying. Many of them had not been pushed this hard since boot camp. We pushed hard on this final hike because at the end of the hike, our students would get fresh fruit, water, their completion certificates, and their bus rides home. We wanted to make sure they not only earned their weekend, but we wanted to make them realize how far they were able to push themselves. This happened every Friday. These hikes were inspirational, and the atmosphere always started off as fun and playful. It was a great way to end the week and the students were thrilled to be marching back to their buses. The jubilant atmosphere did not last long, however. About three-quarters of the way through, the morale would drop almost instantly, the same place and time, every time.

The biggest mountain on our hike was made up of a series of small hills. Unfortunately, with the way the landscape was laid out, three or four of these hills looked like the top of the mountain. While reaching the top of one hill, the typical student would believe that he had reached the top of the crest and the downhill march would begin. That student would be quickly disappointed, however, as they reached the top of the first hill only to have the rest of the mountain revealed. Without fail, week after week, student after student would reach the top of one of these hills and, upon realizing that there was much more mountain to go, would become disheartened. Our hiking formation would crumble. Students would start to drop out. Students who previously could reach out and touch the pack of the Marine in front of them would quickly let great distance form in between them. Some students would drop their packs and sit down or simply fall to the ground on their knees. Our safety truck would drive through the formation and put students in the back with a corpsman, cold water to drink, and an IV if needed. It should be said that not every Marine struggled with this. Some did great, but overall, I knew this series of hills that made up a large mountain was where I was going to start losing our formation and many of our students. This happened every Friday, in the same spot. I and my fellow instructors grew to expect this.

One Friday, however, I thought I would try something new. I made an adjustment. I told the students what the terrain looked like. I told them that we would be going up a series of incredibly steep hills and when we got to the top of each on those hills, although it may look like we have crested the mountain, they were to keep their heads down and keep pushing because there was another incline after that one, and then another. I told them that fourth hill we would go up actually is the top of the mountain, and once we reached the peak, our hike would be all downhill from there. Their buses would be in sight at the foot of the mountains. We tried to manage their expectations, but we were off.

This particular hike started off just like all of them. The students were in good spirits and happy to be headed home. One of their senior leaders would occasionally sing out a marching cadence for the students to repeat. They were wet, tired, and smelly, but they were on their way home.

As we got to the foot of the hills that made up the large mountain, we instructors told them that this was it. We told them that they had four of these bad boys to conquer, so they should fix their minds now. We told them to dig down and conquer that first small hill and let that motivate them to conquer the next, and then the next. We tried to paint the best picture we could of the trail that lay ahead and to use each victory as fuel to keep going to the top of the next hill.

I would watch them. I would watch their faces. They were stoic and confident. They knew what lay ahead. When we got to the foot of first hill, the Marines would grow silent. They would lean forward, breathe, and dig in their heels. When they got to the top of that hill, they would do the same. Some would actually speed up just to keep a tighter formation together. The mere fact that they were focused on the small hill in front of them, and then the next small hill, and the next, made the mountain in front of them much more manageable. They did not psych themselves out by looking at the huge mountain or grow disenchanted when they realized that they had not yet crested the top. They were mentally and physically able to hold it together when they knew about the terrain around them, and the small hills they needed to conquer in order to make it to the top of the mountain. The results were amazing. I cannot say that across the board we lost no Marines on that mountain, but the vast majority of our hiking formation stayed together. It was the power of managing one's expectations and curing one's false illusions. It was the power of small victories that led them to the top of the mountain. The Marines were not encouraged to conquer the mountain in front of them. They were encouraged to conquer the small hill. Then the next . . . then the next. At the crest, they were able to look down and think, *Wow. I just slayed that mountain.* C. H. Spurgeon once colorfully preached, "By perseverance, the snail reached the ark."[6]

I thought I had surrendered my life to Christ once at a church camp in central Oklahoma. Lewis reminded me the opposite. Following Christ is an active, ongoing, daily choice of surrender, and even if we are not conquering the mountain in front of us today, being found in the resistance is a sheer sign that we have surrendered that day to him. This is beautiful because it means that even if yesterday was an abysmal failure, we are not reneging on a one-time commitment that we made to follow Christ long ago. It means today is a brand-new day to pick up our cross again and follow him. His mercies begin new every day,[7] and today is a day that we can get right. One day, with enough small victories under our belt, we will hold our head up high and realize we have made it to the top of the mountain. We can finally drop our heavy pack. Going further up and further in, we will leave the pesky realm of the Shadowlands for good, and with that, the sinful nature that has so often disrupted our relationship with our Creator.

One of my favorite moments in *The Lord of the Rings* by J. R. R. Tolkien is the Battle of Hornburg. During this battle, thousands of Orcs and Uruk-hai storm the garrison of Helm's Deep that is serving as a refuge for the people of Rohan. The residents of this beautiful grassland are primarily herdsmen and farmers. They are easily outnumbered and outmatched on the field of battle. While this battle certainly does take a toll on them, for quite some time the men of Rohan stand their ground and continue to resist with a barrage of arrows and stones hurtling towards the enemy. They are undoubtedly under siege yet are resolute in their resistance.

Eventually however, as the battle grows ever more bloody and ever more dire, after hours of intense resistance, the men begin a retreat deep into the fortress of Helm's Deep. Hundreds of Orc ladders begin to breach the high walls of the fortress and the enemy is soon flooding past Rohan's defenses. Defeat seems inevitable. The Kingdom of Men is failing, and everyone knows it.

In a moment of determination, the Rohan army, led by Aragorn and King Théoden, decides to go down swinging. They fall on the battlefield in

6. Spurgeon, *Salt-Cellars*, 186.

7. Lam 3:23.

complete defiance of the enemy. The Horn of Helm is sounded, and the men of Rohan mount their horses and courageously ride into an onslaught of enemies, swinging their swords along the way. Their demise will be imminent, but they can only hope to bring as many Orcs and Uruk-hai as possible down with them. Hand-to-hand combat soon ensues, and the battlefield becomes littered with casualties. The Kingdom of Man is in full resistance. They may lose, but it is not without swords blazing.

It is then, when sunlight first touches the shadows of the hills towering over the battlefield, that almost all hope is lost. It is when the casualties of Rohan are at their greatest. Aragorn looks up and to the east. What do his eyes behold breaking the ridgeline? He sees Gandalf the White riding a white horse with thousands of reinforcements behind him. A great roar of celebration bellows from the men of Rohan. As Gandalf shines his white light into the eyes of the enemy, they charge the battlefield in a beautiful rescue mission. The army of the Orcs and Uruk-hai at the Battle of Hornburg is decimated soon thereafter. The men have resisted and battled for what almost certainly feels like an eternity to them. Although they are bruised and although they are battle-worn, they are eventually rescued by Gandalf the White.

We may battle our whole lives. We may battle with addiction our whole lives. We may battle with doubt and questions our whole lives. We may battle with pride, materialism, or envy our whole lives. We may battle with any number of vices our whole lives, but as long as the battle remains, as long as the fight continues, as long as we are in the resistance, take heart, the battle continues . . . the reinforcements are on their way. The rescue is coming. One day we too will hold up our heads in the middle of the battlefield, look towards the east at daybreak, and see the Savior, riding on a white horse, coming to rescue his people . . . no matter how dirty they are . . . no matter how battle-worn. They will indeed be rescued.

Lewis writes in *The Weight of Glory*, "Failure will be forgiven; it is acquiescence that is fatal." [8] He goes on to define acquiescence as anything in ourselves that we claim for our own. In other words, every failure on the field of battle will be forgiven. It is complete surrender to the enemy that is catastrophic. On this side of eternity, we may never drive out that enemy. But we have to be found in the "Resistance." [9] We may be found embattled,

8. Lewis, "Weight of Glory," 192.
9. Lewis, "Weight of Glory," 192.

broken, bruised, and bleeding, but we must still be found in the Resistance. And this fight, whether we will win the day or lose the day, must, as Lewis points out, begin again every day.[10]

10. Lewis, "Weight of Glory," 192.

PART 6

Essays on Freedom

20

What the Bird Said

"the holidays have begun. The dream is ended: this is morning."
—Aslan, *The Last Battle*[1]

I F we are honest with ourselves, any struggle that we battle with in this life is no real issue for God. If we are able to step back from our crisis du jour, even the most pessimistic of us can be comfortable with the phrase, "God's not worried." Most would also concur with the old adage, "There are no surprises in Heaven." God's not too shaken, or even surprised, by terrorist organizations in the Middle East. God is not pacing back and forth about elections in the United States. The stock market does not keep him awake at night. So why is it that we act as though our personal struggles shake God, surprise him, cause him to pace, or keep him up at night? When we're intellectually honest, we know that the debts that we owe the bank will not matter in a hundred years, so why is it so easy to think that our spiritual debts will matter? Have they not been paid for? Do we not believe that? We may say we do, but do we live in that reality? Do we relax in it? Being able to grasp this concept is assuredly a powerful step towards freedom.

1. Lewis, *Last Battle*, 210.

They say that combat is 10 percent action and 90 percent boredom. In my experience, this is true. Sometimes in Afghanistan days would go by before we were afforded the opportunity to crawl out of our fighting holes and go on some sort of mission. Sometimes our next mail drop would be a week out. Most of the books I brought, including my Bible, fell apart after the desert heat melted the glue binding. So naturally my friends and I had to come up with some way to entertain ourselves. We stumbled upon a game . . . a very rudimentary game, but a game, nonetheless.

I shared a mortar pit (a big hole in the ground) with my friend Anthony Carter. I love Carter and miss him something awful. He was from the inner-city of Washington, DC and had the best stories. Our unit's mission in Afghanistan was to combat the Taliban, but at times it felt that mine and Carter's mission was to simply make each other laugh . . . and we did a darn good job at it. One day I took a rock out of my fighting hole and tossed it towards an empty ammo can that was a few meters away. I missed at first but tried again until I landed the rock in the can. Since there was no one there to pat me on the back for my accomplishment, I asked Carter to see how many tries it took him. It took him a few tries, but eventually he succeeded too. We continued taking turns back and forth. Like a couple of prehistoric children, our rock game kept our attention for hours.

It didn't take us long, however, until the challenge of tossing a rock a few meters away into an ammo can became too easy, so we decided to add a bit more spice to our challenge. We decided to see if we could get the rock to bounce once and then land in the can. That challenge morphed soon thereafter into making the rock bounce twice and then land in the can. After that, we tried to throw the rock in a way that it would land in the can and bounce directly back out.

Soon, our target grew beyond the ammo can a few meters away to other targets farther in our line of sight. We found targets like rocks and more rocks. We began to give each other outrageous targets like, "Make this rock bounce once on the ground, hit that rock in front of us, and then land in the middle of that circle of rocks." The challenges became more complex, more out of reach. At one point, after accepting an outrageous rock challenge, my friend Carter said, "Man, if you do that, my friend, you are the bomb diggity." And I did just that, and I became the bomb diggity. All of the sudden, our silly little game had a name: the bomb diggity.

Over the course of the next several months in combat, we would challenge each other to rock-tossing challenges that if one was able to complete but the other was not, he had the honor of being bestowed upon him the title of the bomb diggity. I even found a rock suitable for a trophy and wrote *the bomb diggity* on it with a Sharpie . . . I even drew a cartoon-style bowling ball bomb on it. This rock was now the most valued possession in all of Tarinkot.

That trophy made its way back and forth between Carter and me for many months. At times it would even extend to the guns on our left and right. The bomb diggity became an honor, not only to achieve but to retain for days on end.

Often, we would have to change locations quickly, with little notice. We would pack our belongings, fill in our fighting holes, and move out at a moment's notice. After either hiking or riding to our next operating base, ultimately someone would ask, "Did you bring the bomb diggity?" It did not matter our circumstance, as long as we were gathering our food, ammo, weapons, and gear, the bomb diggity was a priority as well. I did not want to be the one responsible for forgetting the coveted trophy at our last location. It's amazing how passionate we can become towards something so cheap and insignificant when we attribute more value to it than it deserves.

Towards the end of our deployment, the powers that be started giving us possible ship-out dates. These were the dates we were told a C-130 was going to land on the makeshift dirt runway we created and take us home. However, if I could go back and talk to the sweaty, young man in his fighting hole, that would one day be writing this essay, I would tell him to "go ahead and just ignore the first several ship-out dates. They will be of no use to you." We got extended several times . . . often on the day we were supposed to leave.

So naturally, when we got the real call to clean our trash, pack up, fill our holes, and make our way down to the landing strip, we were beyond ecstatic. We had been waiting on this day for months on end, and it was finally here.

I cannot say I was nostalgic about leaving the country I had spent so much time and energy in, where I had experienced some extreme highs and some dreadfully low lows. I didn't take a moment to breathe the air one more time or stand at the top of our hill and take it all in one last time. I tightened my pack and followed my squad leader down the landing strip, ready to go home.

It took us a while to get home of course. We had to spend a couple weeks in Kuwait, waiting on our ship. We had to stop in Spain to clean our gear and have a few days of decompression. We had to make the long trek across the Atlantic to the Carolina coast where a hovercraft would take us from ship to shore. From there, we took Chinook helicopters from the shore to our base, and then we were bussed to our camp where our families awaited us.

I did not think about it until the days afterwards. We were unpacked and cleaned up. We got to spend some time with our families back home and then eventually made our way back to our base in North Carolina to get back to training. But a few days of being home from our deployment I realized that I had forgot something in the deserts of Tarinkot, Afghanistan . . . the bomb diggity.

If I had forgotten the bomb diggity when we were moving all around the Urozgan province back in "the 'Ghan," you'd better believe there would be hell to pay . . . or at the very least, ridicule and disdain. But back in the States? It didn't matter a single bit. While in combat, where we experienced only little nuggets of joy and laughter here and there, the bomb diggity trophy was something so prestigious, something to be sought. It was something to be cherished and valued. But when we were back home with our families? The bomb diggity was just a stupid rock. It was of very little value. The title of bomb diggity was left in the desert and no longer mattered. I certainly believed it mattered for a time and period, and certainly put a lot of effort toward achieving it. But back home, those efforts were futile. Looking back, I'm not in the least bit upset that the bomb diggity trophy did not make it back with me . . . it's just a rock.

It makes me wonder what things we are holding of value now that will one day be useless. I imagine quite a bit. Not everything, but I'd wager to say the majority of what we spend our time caring and worrying about will one day soon be completely worthless . . . a distant memory that is only worth chuckling about. It won't be too long until our bank account will seem like nothing more than a rock we left in the desert. One day, our position, our title, and our job will all be nothing but stone trophies buried in a fighting hole. The relationships that broke us; the arrest record that haunted us; the degrees we slaved to earn; even our moral scorecard that we strived to keep and display: these may all have played an important part for a time and a place, but one day soon they will all be the bomb diggity . . . and they won't matter a bit.

⌒

Moral scorecards can build a person up or break a person down. They can reassure someone of their standing with God or make them believe the worst. They can blind someone to their need for a savior or send them to the foot of cross in repentance. They can be a badge of honor or a source of low spiritual self-esteem.

Regardless, whether it brings out the best in us or brings out the worst, one day we are going all going to look back and see that our moral failures and moral achievements were nothing to grasp on to, nothing to feel pride about, nothing to feel shame about . . . nothing but a pile of rocks.

Moral scorecards may be beneficial now, in that they bring us to the cross of Christ, but after we step out of the Shadowlands and into the new holiday, we will realize how poor those scorecards actually are compared to where they need to be; they are not worth more than a stone in the desert. Those who hold their moral scorecard up in the air today for all to see—drawing their identity from it, their sense of being, and their religion—will quickly realize how worthless that card is upon coming home. The only thing that will matter when the author steps onto the stage will be what Christ did on the cross, and how we respond to the light that we have been given.

In *Mere Christianity* Lewis reminds us that we are going to live forever if Christianity is true. That is a fact that is either true or false. There is no in-between. No grey area. No room to be wishy-washy. If it is false, there are several things that we shouldn't bother with given that our life expectancy, at best, is seventy to eighty years—other people being the least of our problems. If it's true, however, there is a great deal that we should worry about if we are going to live for an eternity.[2] The cross of Christ, how we respond to what God lays on our heart, how we treat others, and how we treat the marginalized are among the things that we should bother about. They are eternal. But everything else that we spend so much time, energy, pride, and worry over will one day soon be nothing but a bunch of useless trophies in some distant country that we shall never return to.

Addison's Walk, Magdalene College

On a Saturday evening, September 19, 1931, "Jack" Lewis, his good friend J. R. R. Tolkien, and Hugo Dyson took a stroll down Addison's Walk, a scenic nature walk on the grounds of Magdalene College at Oxford. They had just had dinner and were ready for some great conversation. The topic of conversation? Myth vs. reality. They discussed the Northern Myths of great courage and those of the Nordic gods laying down their lives in a sacrifice to save their people. The skeptical Lewis had no idea what he was getting himself into.

2. Lewis, *Mere Christianity*, 74.

Soon, as the three lovers of literature continued their stroll, Tolkien, the devout Catholic, and Dyson, also a committed Christian, were able to somewhat convince Lewis that courage like those great stories told of did actually exist. In fact, all of the great stories and myths that these literature connoisseurs had grown to love had some hints of the truth. Why does charity make so much sense when it is so countercultural to what we believe? Why does the idea of the innocent laying down his or her life to save the guilty seem so alluring, and make for the greatest stories? Why does a god giving up his splendor to become poor and meek and breakable resound so deeply at our core? Because all these myths contain some truths about the one true myth that was lived out on the platform of history. When we hear a truth, although we may not be able to connect the dots to the real truth, it resonates. Something deep down tells us that we've connected with something real. The story of the innocent Jesus, laying aside his godhood, being nailed to a cross by his own creation in order to save those whom he loved, was a true myth that all stories, myths, and religions had contained bits and pieces of, until it was played out on the stage of history. That was the topic of conversation that these three Oxford Dons were engaged in as they smoked, laughed, and enjoyed one another's friendship.

Lewis had become a theist up until this point but had not stepped over the line and admitted Christ to be his savior. It was this conversation, having gone on well into the night, that was a catalyst for Lewis's conversion to Christianity—one of the most influential conversations that happened in the twentieth century. The ripple effects are still moving forward today.

I walked on that path. It was just as one would have imagined. It looked like something out of Hobbiton: the towering trees that hung just above our heads, providing perfect shade to our path; the stream that twisted and turned seamlessly alongside the path; the stone bridges with the punting boats tied up closely to the edge of the water. Deer grazed the fields to my right. Flowers bloomed by the side of the trail on my left. It was the perfect place to discuss the validation of the Christian story. To think. To mediate. To pray. To wonder.

Oxford, to my surprise did not contain a whole lot of tributes to Lewis. It may be because they are trying to keep the integrity of a wonderful institution and do not want to make their fine school anymore of a mecca for tourists than it already is, or it could be that the institution is still not interested in promoting a man who bucked the system back in the thirties and forties with his popular Christian books. Regardless, there were a few tributes and points of interest for Lewis fans, but not many. I saw much more Harry Potter merchandise in the downtown shops than I did *Narnia* or *The Lord of the Rings* . . . but I suppose that makes sense. Harry Potter is wonderful too.

Our professor did lead us to one, however. It was a little stone memorial on Addison's Walk that I was happy Magdalene College had put in place. It was a poem that had some green moss stains over it, but it was still legible. It was simple. It was sweet. It was powerful. In silence we listened to the birds sing and absorbed this poem on a little stone bridge during Addison's Walk:

What the Bird Said, Early in the Year

I heard in Addison's Walk a bird sing clear:

This year the summer will come true. This year. This year.

Winds will not strip the blossom from the apple trees

This year, nor want of rain destroy the peas.

This year time's nature will no more defeat you,

Nor all the promised moments in their passing cheat you.

This time they will not lead you round and back

To Autumn, one year older, by the well-worn track.

This year, this year, as all these flowers foretell,

We shall escape the circle and undo the spell.

Often deceived, yet open once again your heart,

Quick, quick, quick, quick!—the gates are drawn apart.

I stood there, breathed it in and thought, it does not matter our struggles today. It does not matter the mistakes we are trying to overcome right now or the mistakes we will have to overcome tomorrow. It doesn't matter what we are addicted to currently, or the addictions that await us in our future. It does not matter our entanglements in this world today or what kind of money or materials currently make up our inflated sense of self-worth. It does not matter who broke our heart or what our credit score was. The winter is almost over. Summer is on its way. Flowers are beginning to bloom. Soon blossoms will remain on the apple tree. They will never fall. The winter spell will be broken. The gates will be open. Quick, quick! Let us enter together. Remember . . . when Alsan is on the move, the ice begins to melt. One day, summer will arrive. We'll climb the hill. We'll drop our packs. We'll enjoy our Creator.

I imagine when we finally see Jesus face to face, it will be a very fulfilling experience. When we look towards the east at the break of dawn and our eyes meet our little existence that we were so caught up in, the joy and the pain we've experienced, it will finally make sense . . . in an instant. No words needed. Everything we left behind, including our possessions, our jobs, our politics, and our moral scorecards will be nothing but a fuzzy dream that we may not be sure was real.

It will be like the final piece of a puzzle sliding into place, revealing a beautiful picture. We'll finally have that fulfillment that we've all been trying to obtain through fruitless ventures, relationship after relationship, and endless wanderings from jobs, hobbies, and experiences. When we're finally able to embrace him, the drunk man will realize what he was *really* searching for at the bottom of the bottle and what would have *ultimately* fulfilled his thirst long ago. The promiscuous girl will realize what kind of relationship she was *really* trying to find and be fulfilled by. The rich family will realize what they were really created to value and understand why their money and possessions never made them feel complete. They'll not only feel fulfilled; they'll feel forgiven and restored. In one beautiful instant, every soul will feel their worth.

Every one of us, with our different personalities, sins of choice, and our different means of trying to fill the gap that was created when man separated himself from God, will finally be made whole. The longing we all are experiencing now will be erased with one embrace of our Creator. We will finally be able to bask in perfect union with him. We'll be in perfect union with what we're all currently trying to reconnect with now. It will all just make instant sense.

Lewis used to make the point that one of the reasons he knew that there was a God, and that we were created to one day be fulfilled by that God, is the fact that there is nothing on this earth that is completely and utterly satisfying. No matter what, our ventures we are always left with the sensation that there is something missing . . . something not quite right.

A man's hunger testifies that he was created to be satisfied by food. Although food may or may not be readily available, it suggests that food does in fact exist somewhere, and it does satisfy. Our souls hunger for something completely satisfying. This suggests that there is something out there that does in fact satisfy completely—that will fill in all the gaps of our heart, and we will no longer know what it means to long. I like that. I think it's beautifully true.

I hope I'm on earth when Jesus descends in glory . . . when he returns to the mess we've inevitably created . . . when he waves a flag in the air and says, "Enough is enough." I would love to be a part of the massive crowd of humanity that watches him return to claim his bride. I think he'll probably make eye contact with everyone. It will either be the most fulfilling moment in the history of history . . . or the most dreadful.

I think when he makes eye contact with me, whether descending in glory from the clouds or on the shores of some glorious beach in heaven, I will not recognize him as the Jesus from all the Bible stories. I won't see the handsome white guy my Sunday school teacher used to stick on a piece of flannelgraph. I don't think I'll see the man who turned water into wine or healed the lepers. I don't even believe I'll see the Jesus that hung on the cross or the One that walked out of the grave three days later.

I'm going to see the Jesus I clung to when my life was falling apart. I'm going to see the comforter who held me when I was in tears on the other side of the planet, helpless to save my son's family. I'm going to see the Savior I crawled to night after night after abusing my body with unhealthy substances. I'm going to be able to put a face to the recipient of my prayers . . . who picked me up from the cold hard floors of failure and told me I was still worth something . . . even though I convinced myself I was not. I'm going to see the strong tower I ran to during the loneliest points of my life. When I gaze into the deep wells of love that make up my Savior's eyes, I believe it will be the most personal experience I've ever had. It will click like nothing has ever clicked before. I won't see a stranger. I will recognize a friend . . . a friend whom I have loved and hurt, and by whom I was reassured throughout my troublesome existence on this earth.

I imagine that all those thoughts will occur, but they will occur in an instant, and I will immediately find myself face-down in the dirt. The most surreal sensation of unworthiness will come upon me. I can only hope he'll walk over to me, pull me up, embrace me, and tell me how proud of me he is and how he's longed for this moment too. He'll tell me that he loves me, but more than that, he'll tell me that he is proud of me, that he actually likes me, and looks forward spending an eternity with me . . . at least I hope that's what happens.

Maybe I'm way off . . . and that's ok. But something tells me when we're finally united with Jesus, when the haziness of this dream world clears up and we awaken to our reality, with no more static on the line of our relationship, worshiping him for a million years may very well seem an appropriate and a fulfilling experience—the only experience that we've been created to be fulfilled by.

21

Wait, Be Vulnerable

To love and admire anything outside yourself is to take one step away from utter spiritual ruin.

—C. S. Lewis, *Mere Christianity*[1]

I've probably gained more insight from my relationships with my friends in prison than they have from me. Some of the best advice I have ever received has come from some people who will never step foot back into the free world. I think I travel out to those facilities to do them a service, but I often find that I am the one whose spirit is uplifted.

Not long ago I was writing to my good friend Curtis. I met Curtis in a prison in Oklahoma, and we hit off our friendship very quickly. We had been going back and forth about a range of topics. I was filling him in on several different aspects of my life, updating him on the status of my current dating life, or lack thereof, and he was filling me in on his. Found in his reply, among his many words of wisdom, he dropped a phrase that I've heard a million times. It's a platitude that typically goes in one ear and out the other. It's a phrase that I've even told others in regard to their dating life, yet at times have struggled to apply to myself. He said, "To find the right one, you have to become the right one."

I know this. However, the more I thought about it, especially coming from Curtis, the more it made sense. He was living this out, just in a different way. You see, Curtis was going to be getting out of prison in less than a year, and he just got moved to his last destination before his release: a

1. Lewis, *Mere Christianity*, 108.

minimum-security prison in southeastern Oklahoma. It was a much more peaceful environment than he was used to. There was no fence, just green hills, forests lakes, and wildlife. Many people end up here after decades of serving hard time. It's their final stop before going home and, ideally, saying goodbye to the criminal justice system forever. It is filled with short-timers who are ready to get out. The atmosphere of this facility was different from the others, Curtis told me There were fewer programs and fewer rehabilitation classes. Inmates were not focused on bettering the day-to-day life of the facility. Their focus was shifted towards their imminent future. They start checking off days on the calendar and counting down how many more trips to the chow hall it would be until they went home. In fact, these types of facilities may even prove harder for a church ministry to make a large impact because there are so many inmates there who are checked out and just ready to go home. Their freedom, for understandable reasons, becomes their immediate and only focus.

Here it would be easy for Curtis to relax, watch the clock, and ease back into the real world. If it were me, that's what I would probably do. I'd be very tempted to ride out my last few months on autopilot, waiting for the moment that the guard opens my cell for the last time, and I get the heck out of there . . . but that's not what Curtis did with his last year.

Instead of counting down how many more times he had to wake up in that place, he treated his final year in prison just like every year prior. He started new outreach programs. He played his guitar and sang in the chapel service. He asked me about possibly starting new ministries down there. He studied for his electrician's license. He did a number of things to better himself besides sleeping, eating, and waiting to get out. Yes, the day eventually came when he was handed a pair of civilian clothes and led to the front offices to process out, but in his last year his focus was on bettering himself and deepening his relationship with God. Why? Because Curtis knew his freedom did not come from the outside. Being out of prison was certainly going to be a wonderful thing, but his freedom comes from his relationship with Christ alone, not from his physical address.

Often, people like me get very obsessive. We get caught up on the one thing we can't have, and it devours us. We take something good and we use it to destroy ourselves by trying to make it our ultimate. Some people do it with their career. They find their worth and value in their work, and it consumes them. They cannot live without it, and it dictates every aspect of their lives. For some people it's money. Like Gollum and the Ring, desire for wealth ends up changing everything good about a person. Even when they have plenty of it, they need more and more. For some people it's their spouse. Their significant other becomes their practical savior, and they spend their whole lives putting the weight of their soul onto another fallible human being. It normally ends up decimating the relationship, even if it's just on the inside. As Lewis reminds us, "We may give our human loves the unconditional allegiance which we owe only to God. Then they become gods: then they become demons. Then they will destroy us, and also destroy themselves."[2] We often take really good things and try to squeeze our redemption out of them. We demand that the things that were simply supposed to be the added bonuses of our existence save us. We thrust our meaning onto them and then we become crushed when they inevitably let us down. We again get lost in the misguided attempts at redemption.

It would have been very easy for Curtis to put the weight of his soul on his freedom. It would be very easy for him to obsess over it, as many people in his situation do. Yet he did not. He focused on the here and now. He focused on what he had, not what he may someday get. He focused on his relationship with God and his relationship with others and, what's even better, he encouraged me to do the same. *To find the right one, you have to become the right one.*

I have often misplaced my focus on things of little spiritual importance. I have often thrust the weight of my soul on people and institutions that were never created to bear such weight. I have often obsessed over my next job instead of rejoicing in the one I was blessed with at the time. I have often worried so much about securing my son's future by earning the right kind of employment and education that I forgot to enjoy him here and now. As far as my dating life, I have often tried to find the right one before I focused on being the right one. These were good things that I made my absolute things. I *needed* all of this stuff, and it sucked the marrow out of it all.

The need to find a partner, or land the right job, or make the right amount of money, much like the need to get out of prison, is a telltale sign that one's fulfillment is coming from the wrong spot. Yes, a marriage will be great one day. Yes, earning a decent paycheck will be satisfying. Yes, the prisoner will want to get out of prison. But the overall yearnings of one's heart will never be fulfilled by such things. Our heart has only one need it's chasing: God. The irony here is once that is in place, when our ultimate in life is God alone, it actually makes one a healthier candidate for a quality relationship. It makes one a more desirable employee and a better parent.

In one of my favorite books and lectures that Timothy Keller has produced, *Counterfeit Gods*, he describes it something like this: imagine a starving person who comes upon a beautiful fruit tree. This guy is not going to take a second to notice its beauty. He won't be able to stand back and

2. Lewis, *Four Loves*, 10.

enjoy it for what it is. He will simply devour it. Stripping it of its fruit and ruining its beauty. Yes, he will temporary be relieved of his cravings, but the tree will be left demolished . . . and he'll be hungry again soon.

But what if a contently full person approaches the same magnificent fruit tree? His appreciation for it will be deeper and more robust. He won't ask, "What can this tree do for me?" He will marvel at the tree's grandeur. He will knock off a cobweb or two. He will take a selfie with it and post it on social media. He will be much happier with the fruit tree than the starving man would. Why? Because his fulfillment came from somewhere else, not the tree. If our fulfillment is coming from God, when the right person shows up in our lives, either tomorrow or five years from now, the odds of that relationship working are tremendous. No one will be putting the weight of their soul on another human being, hoping for fulfillment.

One's relationship with a future spouse will be immensely more meaningful and beautiful if one does not *need* it when it arrives. A parent's relationship with their child will be so much more substantial if the weight of that parent's soul is not on the child. An employee will be much more productive and focused if his or her job does not define who they are. The inmate will be able to enjoy their time both inside of prison and outside of prison more if they know that their true freedom is not determined by razor wire. We will be able to enjoy these things on a level that the starving man never could, if our fulfillment comes from elsewhere.

This is often hard because our hearts need to be attached to something. We need to be living for something, earning something, transfixed with something. Everyone you have ever met is living for something. They are attempting to squeeze their worth and their value out of something. Our hearts need to be attached somewhere. I once heard Timothy Keller talk about Scottish theologian Thomas Chalmers. Chalmers wrote a book called *The Expulsive Power of a New Affection*. In it he says that the human heart is such that one can never simply stop a yearning, an addiction, or fascination . . . one can only replace it. If an addict wants to stop *needing* the focus of their addiction, they can't simply stop desiring it. The only way to break that need is to replace it with something else. They have to set the heart on something else. When we find ourselves with a seemingly unhealthy desire, the solution is not to simply stop desiring it. The solution is to replace that desire with something much better.

So, in short, if we try *needing* an intimate relationship with God more than we *need* a romantic relationship with a person, we will appreciate both God and that person so much more when he or she arrives, and we will be in a much healthier position. If an employee needs God more than anything else in this world, their job title will simply be an added bonus, and will probably stand out all the more. If we need Christ more than anything else in this world, everything else will simply be the sugar on top. We will enjoy them more. We will not devour them nor will they devour us. We will complement them, and they will complement us. This is easier said than done and takes time, effort, and failure . . . but it can be done. Remember, I don't want to destroy the fruit tree when it shows up. I want the fruit tree to be a wonderful and beautiful thing, not a source of fulfillment.

Cambridge

At one point during my stay in England, my class and I packed our bags for a few days and headed up to Cambridge where Lewis taught, wrote, and researched from 1954–1960. There are several locations in this small town that any Lewis fan would be encouraged to explore. The Pickerel Inn, which boasts to be the oldest Ale House in Cambridge, dating back to 1608, was the Inkling's extension in Cambridge where Lewis, Tolkien and other members of their elite group of writers and best friends would meet to eat, drink, and continue their discussions of literature, though to a lesser routine than that which took place at The Eagle and Child in Oxford every Tuesday.

There is the large humanities lecture room where Lewis gave his inaugural lecture upon arriving at Cambridge, an event met with so much fanfare and anticipation that not only were students sitting in the aisles once again, but the BBC even considered airing the event live.[3] Unfortunately for us, when we got to this classroom, the lecture room was being used by current Cambridge students and we were unable to go exploring. However, that didn't stop us from sticking our heads through the back door, one at a time, trying not to disturb the occupants who, at the time, could not have cared less about the historical significance of the room as they took notes intently.

Perhaps the most interesting Lewis destination in the city of Cambridge is Magdalene College on the banks of the beautiful River Cam. This was where Lewis settled into his new role at Cambridge and where he finally got the academic recognition he deserved. Lewis lived here after becoming the Chair in Medieval and Renaissance English. This was where Lewis could finally put aside the tiresome tasks of lecturing at the undergraduate level and have the freedom to research and write and, eventually, fall in love with his soon-to-be wife. It was here that he could leave behind the icy relationships that had formed with the English faculty at Oxford, and be embraced by the softer, gentler faculty and students of this smaller, but

3. McGrath, *C. S. Lewis*, 316.

highly regarded, academic institution. After years of getting passed up for promotion, Lewis was finally able to get not only the recognition he deserved but triple the salary. Although Lewis's first love would always be the Kilns (his home in Oxford, which he was still able to keep and live in on the weekends and when the term at Cambridge was not in session), his stay during the week made him happy, more relaxed, and more at peace. That made me happy to be there as well. The move to Cambridge during the week was good for Lewis's mind, body, and spirit . . . let alone his career. He once wrote to a friend about how happy he was that he had moved to Cambridge. Although he was reluctant to take the position at first, he now deemed it was a success. The new college was smaller and softer than the one he had grown accustomed too. He described the mental and social atmosphere as the sunny side of a wall in an old garden. He was finally able to think and relax. He was able to tune out the noise and get a good country walk in. Even his friends told him that he looked younger in Cambridge. He was happy there.[4]

We walked into the courtyard in the middle of Magdalene College and met up with the former archbishop of Canterbury, Rowan Williams. It was drizzling a little bit that morning, so we stepped into the Angelica chapel where C. S. Lewis worshiped at this particular college.

Rowan Williams, apart from being a theologian, a renowned academic, and well, the former archbishop of Canterbury, was also a great fan and student of C. S. Lewis. His book, *The Lion's World: A Journey into the Heart of Narnia*, takes readers on a deep theological study of the world of Narnia that gives a fresh look at Christian doctrine, using Lewis's fictional world—a world where there are no church buildings and no organized religion, just the central figure of Aslan the Great King, who is alone the fulfillment of all the creatures in Narnia.

On a side note, our experience with Archbishop Williams is case in point why taking notes and journaling is of such great importance, especially during once-in-a-lifetime experiences like these. I remember sitting there in the uncomfortable wooden pews of an Anglican church, being mesmerized by the historical legend right in front of me—and while I do remember being overwhelmed and inspired by the words of the great Rowan Williams, as I write this, I cannot remember what he spoke about. I probably shouldn't add such a failure of the mind in a book that will be published one day. But nevertheless, I am embarrassed to say that, while I was deeply moved and in awe of the lecture he gave to his fellow C. S. Lewis admirers, I did not have the presence of mind enough to journal my memories before they

---

4. Lewis, *Letters of C. S. Lewis*, 577.

slipped away. One lesson Rowan Williams did leave me with is to take notes. Journal. Don't let important memories get away.

After hearing from Rowan Williams, our class left the chapel and walked up a set of narrow, circular stairs to the office of the current chaplain of Magdalene College. Unfortunately, the chaplain was out, but he had given us permission to be there. This was an important stop for this band of traveling Lewis students because, besides being the office of the current chaplain, this was the former office of the first chair of medieval and Renaissance English at Cambridge University, Mr. Clive Staples Lewis.

As one would expect, much of the office had been updated, but Cambridge took great care to keep a sizable portion of his office original, true to the famous occupant who used to read, write, and research there. One entire wall was filled with books. This was where Lewis would have kept his impressive collection of literature, a collection so vast that it filled an entire bedroom at his home in Oxford upon his stepping down from chair at Cambridge.

I was drawn, however, to the fireplace where two chairs sat on either side. These chairs were original to Lewis's office. We were told that the brownish-yellow one was Lewis's personal chair. It was worn with age obviously, but something told me this chair was never that beautiful in the first place, but perhaps puke-brown polyester was easier on the eyes in the mid-twentieth century. I sat in it. I thought about the works that Lewis contributed to literature late in his life, and what wonderful ideas came from this chair, this fireplace, and a pipe that was sure to have been puffed at this very spot. This was the spot where Lewis may have revisited the myth of Cupid and Psyche and decided to retell it in his now classic *Till We Have Faces*. This was where Lewis very well may have done his early morning Scripture reading and was inspired to write *Reflections on the Psalms*.

This particular chair also had a unique feature. Attached to it was a contraption I had never seen before. It was a metal arm that had a series of bends and hinges on it that allowed the chair's occupant to clamp a book into place and swing it into a comfortable reading position. It was clunky, but it was functional. Definitely something that looks like it came from the late 1800s or early 1900s. I actually envied it and thought about how much I could use a similar contraption.

This chair seemed to have sat lower than a man of Lewis's age would have been comfortable in at that time. I grabbed the clunky metal arm and swung the book in front of me. It was a Bible—dusty, ragged, pages barely holding onto the binding. It was open coincidentally to the book of Jeremiah. In front of this fireplace, this beat-up, rugged chair was likely the spot where Lewis was free to use his imagination and produce many of the beloved works that came about later in his career. It was here that perhaps Lewis read the letters of Joy Davidman, reminding him that he was never too old to fall in love or dream a new dream.

Lewis's life reminds us that age is no barrier to love. In fact, it often enhances the love that may come. Lewis could have easily settled for any girl whose eye he caught in Oxford at one of the local pubs. He most likely would have had several adoring female fans who he could have used his celebrity status to impress. He could have easily chosen one of his female students at Oxford to kindle a relationship, a practice that was surprisingly common at the time, one Lewis protectively set up boundaries against. Lewis could have settled in any number of ways, but he chose to wait. He chose to wait until the right woman came who challenged his thinking and enhanced his career and talents instead of tearing them down. Joy spurred his thinking and overall complemented the whole of Lewis. He had to wait till late in his life, but I can confidently say that Lewis would have agreed that it was worth it. He did not need a relationship when it found him, so when it did find him it was a blessing.

If Lewis would not have waited to fall in love, I do not think we would know Lewis the way we do today. Not only did Joy Davidman enhance his life while Lewis was alive, albeit short and sweet, her relationship with Lewis spurred on many works we enjoy today. *Till We Have Faces* was encouraged by and dedicated to Lewis's wife. *A Grief Observed*, although somber and the circumstances surrounding it tragic, has inspired and counseled millions of readers, including me. Lewis's relationship with one of his stepchildren (a beautiful relationship not given the attention it's due in my opinion) incited the Lewis brand that we enjoy today on our bookshelves and on our movie screens. If one is more concerned with getting married than they are marrying the right one, they just may miss out on the best that God has in store for them. That's not to say that God won't honor and bless and lift up any marriage. We know he's quite the fan of a godly commitment to one another. But if C. S. Lewis would have settled for the quick fix early in his life, I believe we'd have a very different Lewis to read about and be inspired by today.

That chair in Oxford, Lewis's office, and Lewis's church across the street from Lewis's pub all reminded me that it's OK to wait. God is not bothered by timing. He is not looking at the clock, sweating that time will run out. Whether it is the perfect spouse, the perfect job, the perfect child, the perfect paycheck, it is OK to wait. We can be fulfilled right here and now. We can focus on our relationship with Christ and focus on being a blessing to others. We can focus on becoming the right one before we focus on finding the right one.

I like that chair at Magdalene College in Cambridge. I like that school. I love the historic Pickerel Inn. I love what was inspired by this beautiful market town. I love the fact that Lewis was fulfilled by his relationships with his friends and his relationship with Christ so much so that he never proactively searched for a spouse to fulfill any need that he might have. Here at Cambridge, he was simply enjoying life and chasing after God . . . and one day, he looked to his side and saw a brilliant woman who was chasing after that same God. They grabbed each other's hand and kept chasing him. I love that he never thought that he may be too old to fall in love. Bitterness did not define this old man—indeed, a love of God and love of others did. It was in this small town that Lewis lectured and writes:

> There is no safe investment. To love at all is to be vulnerable. Love anything and your heart will be wrung and possibly broken. If you want to make sure of keeping it intact you must give it to no one, not even an animal . . . Lock it up safe in the casket or coffin of your selfishness. But in that casket, safe, dark, motionless, airless, it will change. It will not be broken; it will become unbreakable, impenetrable, irredeemable. To love is to be vulnerable.[5]

5. Lewis, *Four Loves*, 155–56.

22

Enjoy

No Creature that deserved Redemption would need to be redeemed. They that are whole need not the physician. Christ died for men precisely because men are not worth dying for: to make them worth it.

—C. S. LEWIS, "RELIGION AND ROCKETRY"[1]

I REMEMBER I went through a period where I really wanted to lose some weight. So, I started a regimen of a healthy diet, cardio, and strength training. I eventually achieved my target goal, but I have to say it was a little more mentally draining than I had prepared for. One of my problems was that I was checking my weight every day. Every day I would get on the scale to measure my progress and would sometimes be surprised by my loss, but I would often be let down. Sometimes I would weigh less than the day before, other times, depending on any muscle mass I may have gained or my sodium intake the day prior, the numbers would actually go up. This was disheartening because in my mind I had really thought I was doing a lot better than the scale was saying, yet when I looked down at those little red LED numbers, they would report the opposite. I eventually decided to stop weighing myself and tried to find other ways to track my progress. I started enjoying how much farther I was able to run without losing my breath, or how many more pull-ups I was able to do compared to last time. I started enjoying the way old jeans

1. Lewis, "Religion and Rocketry," (Published as "Will We Lose God in Outer Space" in the April, 1958 issue of *Christian Herald*).

and favorite shirts started to fit again. I started finding positive ways to enjoy my weight loss, rather than stepping on a scale every day.

When I wanted to make an intentional shift from a life spent trying not to upset God to a life spent simply enjoying God, I stopped measuring myself every day. I really forced myself to believe that what Christ did on the cross was sufficient to cover all of my mistakes: past, present, and future. Of course, if there was obvious disobedience in my life, I would still bring these to God in repentance, but I stopped stepping on the scale every day to check myself out. I stopped examining all the wrong in my life and stopped thinking about how vast the chasm is between where I am now and where I will be someday. I just simply started to enjoy God. I started thanking him for the fact that I do not have to measure myself every day. I started thanking him that he gave me another day to live and enjoy him. I started going on walks outside just to enjoy his creation. I began looking up at the trees and thinking: *Wow, God. You know how many leaves are on that tree.* I began to enjoy the miracle of my son and how precious it was just to be in his presence. I began to inwardly and outwardly praise him and enjoy him for no other reason than he is God, and he is good. Lewis writes, "I think we delight to praise what we enjoy because the praise not merely expresses but completes the enjoyment . . . Fully to enjoy is to glorify. In commanding us to glorify Him, God is inviting us to enjoy Him,"[2] and that's what I did. Enjoyment was a missing ingredient I was longing for in my relationship with God. So, I simply added it, and I do not always need to have a reason to enjoy him. I just do. With the language of worship written on my heart, I stopped thinking so much about what I needed to cut out or what I needed to add. I just began to simply love God. Lewis's literary hero George MacDonald writes, "Love makes everything lovely; hate concentrates itself on the one thing hated."[3] Being in love with God again meant I was free from the narrow, hate-filled focus of the parts of me that I didn't like. When you're in love with God simply for who he is, and not how well you're doing on the scale, you begin to love more all over the place. You begin to love others more. You begin to love yourself more. You begin to feel that love returned. For the first time in a long time, I felt that God not only loved me, but he liked me too. It felt good.

It was never about me. It was never about me, and my ability to achieve, or my ability to fail. Every time I made it about me whether I was winning or failing, in spiritual victory or complete spiritual failure, I was being prideful to the highest degree. It was always about him, and if I truly believe that, well

---

2. Lewis, *Reflections on Psalms*, 93–94.

3. Lewis, *George MacDonald*, 127.

that is an awful lot of weight off my shoulders. How much lighter, happier, and closer to God I felt when that weight was removed. When I wanted to physically lose weight, I stopped weighing myself every day. When I wanted to lose spiritual weight and grow closer to God, I stopped measuring my success and my failures every day and just began to enjoy him.

One of the most malevolent schemes Screwtape ever suggested that his nephew use on his Christian targets was to get them to "feel" what they were praying for. When they asked for charity, get them to want to feel charitable. If they prayed for courage, get them to try and feel courageous. When they ask for forgiveness, get them to really try and feel forgiven.[4] Why this scheme? Because Screwtape knows that our feelings come and go, and when they go, our trust in God and our trust in the power of prayer will diminish. This is because our feelings are never consistent. They go up and down based on many factors that we have little control over. They are heavily influenced by our day, by our work, by our health, by our relationships, even by our diet and the chemical activities in our brain . . . but the cross is eternal. It does not ebb and flow. It does not change because our moods, our chemical imbalances, or because of the pizza we ate last night. That means forgiveness is just as eternal. It is constant whether we feel it or not. If the cross remains, so does forgiveness. One of the best tactics I've been able to use against the enemy (both spiritual and the enemy in the mirror), is to accept God's forgiveness as eternal fact, regardless of my ever-changing emotions. I trust that his redemptive work is more powerful and more consistent than whatever neurons happen to be firing (or not firing) in my brain. That thought, if lived out daily, will deeply enhance our enjoyment with our Creator.

Holy Trinity Church, Headington Quarry, Oxford

After a quick meal and some darts at the Six Bells Pub in Headington Quarry, a location that Lewis's brother Warnie used to frequent, my fellow classmates and I made our way on foot to the Holy Trinity Church, just a few blocks down the road from the Kilns. We walked through the stone fence to reveal a postcard-esque church. Holy Trinity was built in 1848 and has remained active and in use ever since. The foundation stone was laid by Samuel Wilberforce, who was the son of the famous William Wilberforce, to whom the world owes a great deal of gratitude today for the abolition of the slave trade.

4. Lewis, *Screwtape Letters*, 16-17.

The outside of the church was surrounded by towering trees, filling the scenery with a variety of lush, green textures. The grounds inside the stone fence are peppered with mossy gravestones dating back to the seventeenth century. We walked through this lawn of beauty and history and through the stone arches that made up the entry of the church. To my surprise, the church was open to the public but empty of tourists or employees. It was just a class of about fifteen students or so and our professor. Like the previous church we had visited on this trip, the air was solemn. We spoke in whispers that were quieter than the echoing of our footsteps on the rock floor below. Stain glass windows allowed in colorful beams of light that painted the wooden pews in the center of the sanctuary. Finally, I found it. I had a seat in the wooden pew I had been looking for since I had been in this church. I sat there, with my back straight, as this pew would not allow any other posture, and read the golden plaque in front of me that proclaimed, "Here Worshiped Clive Staples Lewis." I was in his seat. A nostalgic feeling came over me as I surveyed the church around me.

The Church today certainly has its warts, and it's easier to be more critical of that institution than any other. I'm not sure why. I suppose that we expect so much out of Christ's representation on earth, but if the church didn't have its flaws, Christ would not have to have died to purify her. Modern churches may have their share of problems, but that's no different from the churches of old. Indeed, the only reason we have much of the New Testament is because some well-meaning followers of Christ wrote letter after letter to some very troubled churches, trying to iron out their wrinkles. Those churches kept those letters, and we read them today. She has never been without issues. And that's ok.

C. S. Lewis writes to a friend, "we must be regular practicing members of a church, despite the fact that we are different in temperament."[5] He goes on to explain how some people find it more natural to approach God in quiet and solitude. But that cannot be the only way we approach to God. We must go to church as a society of people, with all of our differences, united only as the body of Christ. Lewis knew that we must not be ashamed of those differences but bring them to a God who rejoices in them and has no desire to iron them out. It is precisely because of those differences that we are able to complement one another and help each other out.[6]

I was sitting in the pew where he practiced what he preached. We're all different. God rejoices in our differences and has no plans of making us all the same. The beauty of the body of Christ is that, no matter our color,

5. Lewis, *Letters of C. S. Lewis*, 515.

6. Lewis, *Letters of C. S. Lewis*, 515.

no matter our styles of church, no matter the ways we all individually connect with God, no matter our variety of mistakes, we all unify to worship
one Holy God. The church should have the most diverse makeup of any
population or any people group in the history of humanity. Lewis knew that
we should enjoy all the diversity under God's creation because heaven will
have far more variety than hell.[7] God intended our churches to be rich with
diversity and never competition. We have an eternity to spend with other
people who look and act nothing like us. We might as well get a jump on
that now.

Our professor pointed out how the seat I was sitting in nestled right up
next to a giant stone pillar that supported the ancient ceiling. He told us that
Lewis picked this particular seat for two reasons. For one, it shielded him
from people coming through the front door. As Lewis's fame spread, fans of
his Narnia series and other works were eager to meet him. Lewis was famous
for always taking the time to talk with his fans and maintaining long-lasting
correspondence with them, but apparently when at church, Lewis wanted it
to be just himself and the body of believers in his neighborhood. He hid in
this seat, far from any non-members who came through the door looking
for their favorite children's author. He also chose this seat because it blocked
his view of the priest. Lewis preferred to listen to the priest and absorb the
liturgy without the distraction of what the priest was wearing, looked like,
or how his stage presence was. I thought this was an interesting thought. I
liked it. I wonder if it would work today. I'm a fan of the bells and whistles,
the smoke and lights, but I wonder, if the modern Christian had nothing to
focus on but the gospel, would that suffice? I tend to believe that it would
for many people, but it's a good question to ask ourselves. Regardless, I did
not think about it for very long. It was time to move on, so I stood up, took a
few pictures, and walked past a beautiful etched-glass window above Lewis's
seat that was, appropriately enough, a Narnia-themed window.

We walked outside into the grassy lawn and graveyard that I was happy
to see was not all that well-kept. It was lush with overgrown vegetation.
Many spots were slightly maintained, but overall nature had been allowed
to proceed as it deemed necessary. I always enjoy visiting graveyards for
some reason, especially older ones. I guess it reminds me that one day, not
only will I be gone from this earth, but my body will be six feet under. Soon,
the fresh dirt on top of me will give way to grass and weeds. Within a few
decades, the script on my tombstone will become hard to read. It will be
hard to tell what years I lived or what my name even was. The world will

---

7. Lewis, *Letters to Malcom*, 10.

have moved on. Everyone that knew me and everything I worked for would soon be forgotten.

Old graveyards are a solemn reminder for me to make sure I am living for what counts, to make sure I am living for the eternal—the only thing that will matter when I am a distant memory. One day, back in the Shadow-lands, the only thing that will remember me will be a small stone memorial withering away in a corner of a forgotten graveyard. The only question that will matter is, "Who did I live for?" Did I live for myself, creating a more comfortable world around me, filling it with luxury that has rotted away with me? Or did I live for others? Did I live a life that was bigger than myself, that stretched on into eternity . . . and did I teach my family to do the same? Old graveyards ask me, "Did I live for God?"

I approached a gravesite of a man who did live a life larger than himself. Not only did his personal life scream his faith in God by his generosity—the giving of himself to others, the opening of his home to those who could not look after themselves, and the giving of his time and energy to those who needed his ear—but his professional life did as well—his writings and his books shouted a life lived for God. They have inspired countless believers and nonbelievers alike from the day they were published up until this day, and certainly into the beyond. Here was the grave of a man who by all accounts was a genius, but who also showed that serving God by serving others is not only reserved for the super smart, the resourceful, or the talented. Serving God by serving others is simple. There's no need to complicate things. The least among us is still able to show love to an elderly woman with dementia by preparing her food and walking her dog. The non-educated can still be a consistent force of love and support to a brother who routinely needs extra attention because of his alcoholism. It does not take talent to open one's arms to children with nowhere else to go during a time of war. Serving God is simple. How we love to complicate the simplest of ideas.

Here was the tombstone of a man who took what the religious elite attempted to complicate and put out of reach to the common man and made it simple—on the bottom shelf for all to enjoy. His life stretched beyond this rock and the unkept grass around it, and stretched deep into eternity, deep into the mountains of God. It read:

IN LOVING MEMORY OF
MY BROTHER
CLIVE STAPLES LEWIS

BORN BELFAST 29TH NOVEMBER 1898

DIED IN THE PARISH
22ND NOVEMBER 1963

MEN MUST ENDURE THEIR GOING HENCE

The date of his death may seem familiar to some American readers. When C. S. Lewis collapsed in his downstairs makeshift bedroom, the headlines of his death were overshadowed by the assassination of president John F. Kennedy. At first, looking at that date made me sad. Here was a man who just never really got his dues throughout his life. His mom died at an early age. His relationship with his father was strained to say the least. His best friend died in combat. Lewis himself was wounded in combat. He was constantly taking it on the chin for being a Christian at a secular university, and all the popular, nonacademic books ultimately hurt his career at Oxford. His personal life was constantly wearing on him, and there was always some sort of drama that he needed to attend to at his busy home. When he finally did fall in love and marry, his wife died a few short years after. And here, on the day of his death, very few even knew about it for weeks as it was overshadowed by a horrible tragedy of historic proportions. Make no mistake, it was overshadowed for important reasons. America had lost a fine president. But I thought, *Wow. He couldn't even get the day of his death all to himself.* But, somehow, I do not believe Lewis would have wanted it any other way.

I knelt by the stone that was due for a good cleaning. The moss had advanced across the top of it since the last scrubbing. I thought the line from Shakespeare's *King Lear*, "Men Must Endure Their Going Hence," may make a fan like me sad, but did I actually think it would have bothered Lewis in the least bit? Of course not. In fact, when Lewis's health was failing, he awoke from a twenty-one-hour coma after a heart attack and was actually upset that he had woken up in the Shadowlands. He would have preferred to get on with it, instead of retuning back to a world of financial problems and failing health. Lewis had moved on. He had gotten on with the real life. In *The Last Battle*, the final book in his Narnia series, Lewis concludes his epic masterpiece with this paragraph:

> And as He spoke, He no longer looked to them like a lion; but the things that began to happen after that were so great and beautiful that I cannot write them. And for us this the end of all the stories, and we can most truly say that they all lived happily ever after. But for them it was only the beginning of the real story. All their life in this world and all their adventures in Narnia had only been the cover and the title

page: now at last they were beginning Chapter One of the
Great Story which no one on earth has read: which goes on
for ever: in which every chapter is better than the one before.[8]

Lewis was enjoying God—something he had done his entire life, but
only had barely tasted here in the Shadowlands. That's what is important.
That's the only thing that's important. Lewis reminds us in *The Problem of
Pain* that our soul has a specific shape. We were made with a particular key
to unlock it, and one day our eyes will behold that key. Every bit of us, aside
from that pesky sinful nature, is destined for complete and utter satisfaction, if only we can lay down and let God have his way. Our place in heaven
will be the perfect fit because it was made precisely for us. When we step
into heaven, we will experience a total feeling of completeness. Any longing
we ever had will instantly disappear, because we were made for it and it was
made for us. Like a personalized glove is made for a hand, Lewis says, stitch
by stitch, Heaven was created for us.[9] There, beyond the gates of pearl, our
souls will finally be nestled, comforted, and put at ease.

I placed my hand on the lower right corner of this long gravestone, and
in my head, I said a little prayer. I thanked God that I could enjoy him just
because he was good and that he loved me. I did not feel the need to slay
my sinful nature first. I did not feel the need to clean up first. I did not feel
the need say any kind of particular prayer. I was happy to approach a loving
God just the way I was. I smiled and just enjoyed God; even better, I felt God
enjoyed me too. That was a feeling I had longed to have.

It had been a long time, if ever, that I really felt like God enjoyed me. It
felt good. I was in the churchyard and at the memorial for the man I credited
for reminding me that God does not just love me. He likes me too. He smiles
upon me despite the muck that I allow to get in the way. My soul had come a
long way. I had spent years and years beating my spirit up with self-induced
blows by the sin I toyed with for far too long. I had spent years and years
allowing my small view of God, my fundamentalist, middle-school view of
God, to batter and bruise a soul which could only breathe if it was enjoying and being enjoyed by its loving Creator. By this point, my low spiritual
self-esteem was a faint memory. I had no idea if I was a third-stringer or a
first-stringer. Who cared? I was on his team, and I knew the coach delighted
in me.

I did not set out to purposefully start a three-year Lewis Remedy, and I
certainly didn't mean for it to consummate with a trip to Oxford and Cambridge, but I was certainly glad it happened. All the reading, all the research,

---

8. Lewis, *Last Battle*, 210–11.

9. Lewis, *Problem of Pain*, 152.

all the lectures . . . it was all well worth it. Before I had started on this journey, I was a prideful man with a wounded spirit, convinced that I was chasing after a disappointed God, working alongside and attending church with
first-stringers who had their act together . . . so much more than I could ever
hope for. It was a sad state. It was dark. It was lonely. It was restrictive. But
now . . . now I felt something I knew all along was supposed to accompany
this whole following Christ thing, but I never seemed to possess it until
now: freedom . . . sinful, yet free . . . prone to failure, yet free . . . prone to low
self-esteem, yet free . . . prone to pride, yet free . . . battled, bruised, scared,
and war-torn, yet free . . . and whom the Savior sets free is free indeed.

    I got up. I took my pictures. My friends and I made our way past all
the gravestones, back to the pavement walkway, through the entrance of the
stone fence, and out of the churchyard of Holy Trinity Church. It was quiet.
I had one line in my head walking away from that place that represented so
much life and so much death:

> *I know now, Lord, why you utter no answer. You are yourself*
> *the answer. Before your face questions die away. What other*
> *answer would suffice?*[10]

C. S. Lewis writes of George MacDonald's masterpiece, *Phantastes*, that it
has a certain quality of death, good death, for Lewis's mind. What it did for
him is "convert, even baptize" his imagination.[11] Many can say the same
thing about Lewis's works, including me. The old, miniscule view of God
was put to death. I had detached my relationship with God from our current, regional, way of doing church and allowed it to stand on its own two
legs. A new and strong view of God had emerged, and it felt like a home-
coming. For me, reading Lewis was like reading someone who has decoded
my heart when I myself could not figure out the combination. He invited
me to stop thinking of my failures so much and, along with that, to stop
thinking of myself altogether. The progress report I now hold up says what
Christ has done, not the mistakes I have made. Lewis reminded me that
following Christ means laying down my arms[12]; the battle is over. He reassured me that my mistakes do not make me the monster that I often felt they
did, that surrendering to God sometimes means simply trying again. While

10. Lewis, *Till We Have*, 308.

11. Lewis, *George MacDonald*, XXXIX.

12. Lewis, *Mere Christianity*, 56.

there is often some ground to be gained in my battle against low spiritual self-esteem, my journey with my Lewis Remedy has certainly launched me in the right direction. He helped highlight the freedom that is found in the gospel that I had overlooked for so long. This allowed me to forgive everyone, including my fundamentalist culture, those who have wronged me, but more importantly, I was free to forgive my most recurring and relentless enemy: myself.

Though spiritual ups and down are sure to come, the diabolical self who lies beneath has already been slain on the cross. It is up to me to keep expanding my view of God, to keep shattering and rebuilding that view, to relax, to enjoy, to wonder, to suppose. Let him remove the dragon skin . . . and he has . . . a couple thousand years ago. Who am I to think that I can do a better job accomplishing what Christ already did on the cross? "Forget your pride," Aslan would tell me, "and accept the mercy of these good kings."

> *You too are going through a dreadful time. Ah well, it will not last forever. There will be a day for all of us when "it is finished." God help us all.*
>
> —C. S. Lewis[13]

13. Lewis, *Letters to American*, 64–65.

Bibliography

Apologetics315, "C.S. Lewis Original Recording," accessed June 6, 2012, video, https://www.youtube.com/watch?v=3MgsoWenaro.

Bonhoeffer, Dietrich. *Discipleship*. Minneapolis: Fortress, 2003.

————. *Papers and Letters from Prison: Readers Edition*. Minneapolis: Fortress, 2015.

Chambers, Oswald. *My Utmost for His Highest*. Grand Rapids: Discovery House, 2005.

Downing, David C. *The Most Reluctant Convert: C. S. Lewis's Journey to Faith*. Downers Grove, IL: InterVarsity, 2004.

Keller, Timothy. *Counterfeit Gods*. New York: Penguin, 2011.

————. *The Reason for God: Belief in an Age of Skepticism*. New York: Penguin, 2008.

Lewis, C. S. *The Abolition of Man*. New York: HarperCollins, 2009.

————. "After Priggery—What?" In *Present Concerns*, edited by Walter Hooper, 65–71. New York: HarperOne, 1986.

————. "The Christian View on Suffering." In *Readings for Mediation and Reflection*, edited by Walter Hooper, 103–4. New York: HarperCollins, 1992.

————. *The Chronicles of Narnia: The Horse and His Boy*. New York: HarperOne, 1954.

————. *The Chronicles of Narnia: The Last Battle*. New York: HarperOne, 1956.

————. *The Chronicles of Narnia: The Lion, the Witch and the Wardrobe*. New York: HarperOne, 1982.

————. *The Chronicles of Narnia: Prince Caspian*. New York: HarperOne, 1951.

————. *The Chronicles of Narnia: The Silver Chair*. New York: HarperOne, 1953.

————. *The Chronicles of Narnia: The Voyage of the Dawn Treader*. New York: HarperOne, 1952.

————. "Evil and God." In *God in the Dock*, edited by Walter Hooper, 3–7. Grand Rapids: Eerdmans, 1970.

————. *The Four Loves*. New York: HarperCollins, 1960.

————. *George MacDonald*. New York: HarperCollins, 1946.

————. *The Great Divorce*. New York: HarperCollins, 1946.

————. *A Grief Observed*. New York: HarperCollins, 1961.

————. "The Inner Ring." In *The Weight of Glory*, 141–57. New York: HarperCollins, 1949.

————. *The Letters of C. S. Lewis*. Edited by W. H. Lewis and Walter Hooper. New York: HarperCollins, 1993.

————. *The Letters of C. S. Lewis to Arthur Greeves*. Edited by Walter Hooper. London: Collier, 1979.

———. *Letters to an American Lady*. Edited by Clyde Kilby. Grand Rapids: Eerdmans, 1967.

———. *Letters to Children*. Edited by Lyle W. Dorsett and Marjorie Lamp Mead. New York: Touchstone, 1985.

———. *Letters to Malcolm: Chiefly on Prayer*. New York: Mariner, 1964.

———. *Miracles*. New York: HarperCollins, 1947.

———. *Mere Christianity*. New York: HarperCollins, 1952.

———. *Of Other Worlds: Essays and Stories*. San Diego: Harcourt, 1966.

———. "On Forgiveness." In *The Weight of Glory*, 177–83. New York: HarperCollins, 1949.

———. "On Obstinacy and Belief." In *The World's Last Night, and Other Essays*, 11–30. New York: Harper One, 1955.

———. *The Pilgrim's Regress*. Grand Rapids: Eerdmans, 2004.

———. *The Problem of Pain*. New York: HarperOne, 1940.

———. *Reflections on the Psalms*. New York: HarperOne, 1958.

———. "Religion and Rocketry." In *The World's Last Night, and Other Essays*, 87–98. New York: Harper One, 1955.

———. *The Screwtape Letters*. New York: HarperCollins, 1942.

———. "A Slip of the Tongue." In *The Weight of Glory*, 184–92. New York: HarperCollins, 1949.

———. *Surprised by Joy: The Shape of My Early Life*. New York: HarperOne, 1955.

———. *Till We Have Faces: A Myth Retold*. New York: Harcourt, 1984.

———. "The Weight of Glory." In *The Weight of Glory*, 25–46. New York: HarperCollins, 1949.

———. *Yours, Jack: Spiritual Direction from C. S. Lewis*. Edited by Paul F. Ford. New York: HarperOne, 2008.

Lucado, Max. *Grace: More Than We Deserve, Greater Than We Imagine*. Nashville: Thomas Nelson, 2012.

Martindale, Wayne. *Beyond the Shadowlands*. Wheaton, IL: Crossway, 2005.

McGrath, Alister. *C. S. Lewis—A Life: Eccentric Genius. Reluctant Prophet*. Carol Streams, IL: Tyndale, 2003.

Nouwen, Henri J.M. *In The Name of Jesus*. New York: Crossroad, 1989.

Osborne, Larry. *Accidental Pharisees*. Grand Rapids: Zondervan, 2012.

———.*Spirituality for the Rest of Us*. Colorado Springs: Multnomah, 2007.

Spurgeon, Charles H. *The Salt-Cellars: Being a Collection of Proverbs Together With Homely* Notes. London: Forgotten Books, 2012.

Wirt, Sherwood E. "I Was Decided On—An Interview with C. S. Lewis." *Decision Magazine* September & October 1963. *Knowing and Doing* cslewisinstitue.org. Spring 2006.

Acknowledgments

A HUGE thank you to Crossings Community Church, your staff, your members, and your volunteers. Thank you for all that you have done for me and for my family and thank you for your continued heart for the marginalized in our community.

I owe a huge debt of gratitude to Professors Linda and Robert Banks. Thank you both for believing in me early on and teaching me everything I know about CSL. I would have never attempted to publish a book without your inspiration. More than anything, thank you for your friendship.

A huge thanks to Rene Gutteridge for also believing in me and introducing me to the world of writing. Everyone reading this should Google you and buy all of your books! Thank you as well for your friendship.

To David Young, Darrin Elliott, Lil P, Keith Bonner, Pastor Mac, and all of my friends at Joe Harp, I love all of you guys. You inspire me daily.

To all of my friends and family. Thanks for having patience with me and sticking by me through it all.

Mason, I love you so very much. The greatest honor I've ever had was becoming your Daddy. I'm beyond proud of that title and I'm beyond proud of you. When you discover this page, turn it in to me for a free day of uninterrupted video games.

Index